PLAIN TALK

Lessons from a Business Maverick

KEN IVERSON

with TOM VARIAN

John Wiley & Sons, Inc.

NEW YORK • CHICHESTER • WEINHEIM • BRISBANE • SINGAPORE • TORONTO

Copyright © 1998 by Ken Iverson
Published by John Wiley & Sons, Inc.

This publication is designed to provide accurate and authoritative
information in regard to the subject matter covered. It is sold with
the understanding that the publisher is not engaged in rendering
legal, accounting, or other professional services. If legal advice
or other expert assistance is required, the services of a competent
professional person should be sought.

Library of Congress Cataloging-in-Publication Data:

Iverson, Ken.
    Plain talk : lessons from a business maverick / by Ken Iverson
with Tom Varian.
        p.   cm.
    Includes bibliographical references and index.
    ISBN 0-471-15514-4 (acid-free paper)
    1. Nucor Corporation—History. 2. Steel industry and trade—
United States—Management—Case studies. 3. Industrial
management—United States—Case studies. I. Varian, Tom.
II. Title.
HD9519.N83I94   1998
338.7'669142'0973—dc21   97-30126
                                                           CIP

Printed in the United States of America
10 9 8 7 6 5 4 3 2 1

To my wife, Martha, my children, Claudia and Marc, and to my grandchildren, Kristin, Garrik, Dana, and Eric.

CONTENTS

CONTENTS

FOREWORD

I've written a half-dozen books about Ken Iverson. I didn't *know* I was writing about him. I thought I was writing about leadership. But as I read *Plain Talk*, I realized that Ken is in many ways the leader I've portrayed in the abstract, here in the flesh.

Ken Iverson has intuitively practiced virtually all of what I've preached. I've said, for example, that *"Great leaders instill groups of people with a dream, but it is a dream with a deadline."* Nucor, the business shaped and led by Ken, is infused with an extraordinary mix of lofty aspirations and a dogged determination to get things done.

I've said that, "*Leaders must be social architects who engineer an atmosphere in which creative dissent is welcomed and in which people are willing to take risks.*" I have seen such an atmosphere. It is Nucor. *Plain Talk* takes us on an intimate tour of this constructively candid business culture.

I've said that, "*Militaristic, command-and-control leadership is an anachronism. Making the transition from the old style of leadership to the new one is a challenge for top management at every organization.*" In retrospect, I might have said, ". . . at every organization *except Nucor.*" Over 35 years, Ken has never practiced (nor tolerated) a command-and-control style. In this regard, as in so many others, he and his Nucor colleagues have long exercised a brand of leadership to which others now aspire. Reading Ken's book, in fact, affirmed a wide range of my beliefs on leadership:

"*Today's leader must maintain sensitivity to the views of everyone who has a stake in the company and realize that each one can make a special contribution to meeting the company's goals.*"

"*Good leaders must also be good followers. Leaders and followers share certain characteristics such as listening, collaborating, and working out competitive issues with peers.*"

"*Specialized management is an enemy of hope and good management. I think what we need, if anything, is deep generalists. I think business schools have played into specialization too much. That's a disservice to institutions.*"

As you read *Plain Talk*, reflect on your notion of the ideal leader, then prepare yourself to experience some startling flashes of recognition.

WARREN BENNIS
Distinguished Professor of Business Administration at the Marshall School of Business Administration, USC, and author of Organizing Genius

ACKNOWLEDGMENTS

There are so many I cannot possibly name them all. I need to thank John Wiley & Sons, Inc., for being interested in the book. Jim Childs really was the first to trigger my interest. Renana Meyers has been a great help in getting it ready for publication. Jim Hlavacek was an inspiration in keeping the book moving and in editing out the areas that didn't fit. Tom Varian has somehow taken all the talks, tapes, interviews, and memoranda and come out with a coherent reflection of our philosophy and practices.

I also must acknowledge all the people of Nucor who helped with their interviews and comments. They are really what the book is all about.

PLAIN TALK

INTRODUCTION

M OLTEN METAL is a wild and restless force. Engineers, supervisors, and production workers will gather around a new caster like kids at the lighting of a bonfire, staring in silent expectation while the maiden melt of steel spits and hisses its way through the apparatus. If the caster works, the long rectangular shells of cooling steel will secure the still-molten core, glowing in its persistent fury, and the onlookers, having caged the beast, will clap one another on the back, celebrating their collective triumph over a power not one of them could hope to master alone.

To my eyes, two of the most fascinating sights to behold are hot metal in motion and a group of people in headlong pursuit of a shared purpose. Those images are the essence of Nucor. They convey how we turned a confused, tired old company on the brink of bankruptcy into a star player in the resurgence of American steel.

Along the way, we did something that is probably more consequential for you: We showed that many of the so-called "necessary evils" of life in corporate America are, in fact, not necessary. The people of Nucor stand in sharp, even defiant contrast to the status quo. We're big on informality, caring, freedom, respect, equality, and the simple truth. We have little tolerance for the politics, the pettiness, the fixation on rank and status, and the insensitivity to employees' legitimate needs that people in most big companies endure as a matter of course.

Since I have no special insight into the forces behind what passes for "business as usual" in most large corporations, I won't spend much time trying to explain them. I'll focus instead on presenting an alternative set of assumptions and approaches for running a business. I'll describe how we raised Nucor from obscurity to its current place as America's third-largest steel company, and I'll explore our company's seeming incongruities:

- Our 7,000 employees are the best-paid workers in our industry, yet Nucor has the lowest labor cost per ton of steel produced.

4

- Nucor is a Fortune 500 company with sales in excess of $3.6 billion, yet we have a total of just twenty-two people working at our corporate headquarters, and just four layers of management from the CEO to the front-line worker.

- Nucor operates in a "rust belt" industry that lost one-out-of-two jobs over a twenty-five-year span, yet Nucor has never laid off an employee or shut down a facility for lack of work, nor have we lost money in any business quarter for more than thirty consecutive years.

- We are in a labor-intensive and technology-intensive business, yet we've built most of our manufacturing facilities in areas that have more cows than people.

- We track and manage costs more closely than just about any business you can name, yet we anticipate and accept that roughly half of our investments in new ideas and new technologies will yield no usable results.

- Nucor pays hourly wages and salaries that run about 66 percent to 75 percent of the average for our industry—the rest of our employees' income comes from "at risk" bonuses—yet we regularly have large pools of qualified applicants for every job opening.

- Our company is broken up into 21 independently operated businesses, each with almost complete local autonomy, yet we have an unusually active and free exchange of ideas and solutions across divisional, geographical, and functional boundaries.

- We have no R&D department or corporate engineering group, yet we were America's first major operator of "mini-mills," the first to demonstrate that mini-mills could make flat-rolled steel (a high-end steel product formerly made only by the Big Steel companies), the first to apply thin-slab casting (a technology Big Steel had written off as impractical), and the first to commercially produce iron carbide (an energy-efficient substitute for the scrap metal from which mini-mills make steel).

This is a book about leadership and life, about business and people and honesty and risk-taking and a whole bunch of things that really add up to how to be successful over the long run. The advice I'll offer isn't fool-proof. But it is tested under fire.

When I joined the company in 1962, it was still called Nuclear Corporation of America. Nuclear was a Johnny-come-lately conglomerate fast approaching the end of a long and twisted road.

The company was launched in 1906 as Reo Motor Car by Ransom E. Olds who, having founded Oldsmobile a couple of years earlier, jumped that ship before it was swallowed up by General Motors. Reo Motor Car stayed independent, building cars until 1936 and trucks until 1957, when it sold off the last of its auto and truck manufacturing business.

In 1955, Reo Holding merged with Nuclear Consultants to form Nuclear Corporation of America, which planned to manufacture nuclear instruments and other electronics, and to hire itself out to conduct radiation studies. The field seemed glamorous at the time, but the business never gained much momentum.

By 1962, Nuclear was dabbling in a variety of businesses with no clear purpose. The company made a bid to acquire Coast Metals, my employer at the time, but the deal was rejected by Coast's board of directors. So Nuclear asked me to help them, part time, to identify other companies in the metals business that they might acquire. I was 37 years old and interested in learning how acquisitions worked, so I agreed to do it. When I recommended they acquire Vulcraft, a steel joist manufacturing firm in Florence, South Carolina, Nuclear asked me to go run it for them.

By 1965, the Vulcraft Division was doing well. Steel joists are a key structural component in industrial, commercial, and institutional construction, and there was a pretty good building boom under way. Unfortunately, Nuclear Corporation as a whole was bleeding money, losing roughly $400,000 on annual sales of $20 million. When the company defaulted on two major loan payments, bankruptcy loomed and the president resigned.

The board approached me to take his place. Apparently, managing the only profitable division in the company made me presidential material. Although I was just 39 years old, I wasn't too flattered. No one else wanted the job. It was mine by default.

I soon learned that Nuclear's shareholders had all but given up hope. They assumed the company was a goner, no matter what I did, so the prevailing attitude was, "If it doesn't cost anything, sure, try it." CFO Sam Siegel and I quickly sold off the half of the company that was unprofitable, then set out to build on our profitable base of Vulcraft operations in Florence, South Carolina, and in Norfolk, Nebraska, where Nuclear had built a second joist plant. Our strategy was what executives now call "focusing on our core competencies," although that's not what we called it. We just placed the few chips we had left on the businesses that were turning a buck. In 1966, we moved Nuclear's corporate headquarters from Phoenix, Arizona to Charlotte, North Carolina. In 1968, we integrated backward, from making joists out of steel into making the steel itself, and in 1972 we changed the name of the company to Nucor Corporation.

Today, our company is thriving. Nucor operates eight steel mills that each year produce more than eight million tons of steel sheet, bars, angles, and light structural carbon and alloy steels. Thirteen other Nucor divisions produce joists, steel deck, bolts, bearings, grinding balls, machined steel products, steel fasteners, cold finished steel, iron carbide, and metal buildings. Nucor-Yamato, a joint venture with Yamato Kogyo of Japan, produces wide-flange beams, pilings, and heavy structural steel products.

We're proud of how far we have come but, in truth, the steel products business is just a backdrop for what I wish to share with you. I'd like to offer you a different slant on the world than you may have gotten from your business school, from your own experiences at work, or from management books (of which I am an avid reader). These pages hold no pat leadership formulas, no intricate management models. In the rush of the real world, I've rarely found time for such things. Rather, they present a casual compilation of my experiences and perspectives. I'll describe some of the choices I've made. I'll present the thoughts and perspectives of many of my Nucor colleagues who helped shape our culture. And I'll explain why we at Nucor so often choose paths different from those followed by most corporations.

I have no desire to win converts. I just want to widen the range of "field-tested" options available to all managers as they choose their own paths.

Finally, I hope to capture at least a bit of all I've felt because, lord knows, I've had one heck of a good time.

1

A HIGHER CAUSE

During the first few months of 1982, it seemed like somebody had turned gravity up a couple of notches. The extra weight was there in my step as I walked through a Nucor mill. I could feel it in the pit of my stomach, see it pressing down on the shoulders of the men working on the line, even hear it in their voices.

A crane operator who saw me coming set his levers in neutral, pushed the hard hat back off his forehead, and cupped his hands to yell over the roar of the furnaces: *"Hey, Ken! Know anybody wants to buy some steel?"* So I hollered back, *"Yeah, but I need you to go hold a gun to his head.*" The crane man smiled. I wished I had a better answer for him.

It wasn't gravity pulling us down, of course. It was the economy, which was (as the business writers liked to say) "mired" in a slump, and nobody was mired deeper than the people who made steel and steel products for a living. This was our passage through the darkest hours of a dark era that saw the number of American steel workers plunge from about 400,000 to just 200,000. Some pundits even pronounced that American steel was dead. Small wonder. In Pittsburgh and Johnstown and Erie and Wheeling, mills fell silent and "House For Sale" signs lined working-class streets like tombstones marking the demise of job after job. Seeing all that, you had to wonder if maybe the pundits weren't right. You couldn't help but ask yourself, "Will that happen to *us?*" Not without a fight.

Farther down the line, I bumped into a maintenance man I'd known for fifteen years. We shook hands and asked after one another's families, then he mentioned that he'd had lots of free time, lately, to polish his pool game. "Let's you and me shoot a few racks after my shift. Ten bucks a rack," he suggested. "I could use the money," he added with a self-assured wink. It was the same good-natured ribbing we'd always enjoyed. This time, though, the strain showed clear through his smile. He *could* use the money. Yet, he wanted to laugh about it, and he wanted *me* to laugh, too, because we both felt the weight.

Nucor production was down by nearly half. Why make products when there's nobody to buy them? Cutting back to four-day or even three-day work weeks reduced the average Nucor worker's earnings by 25 percent. You know that had to hurt. Still, as I'd walk through our mills and plants, I never heard one employee complain about it. Not one.

Their equanimity didn't stem from their courage in the face of crisis, although they demonstrated plenty of that. It wasn't from worrying they'd be fired if they complained. The way things were going, the job wouldn't be worth a plug nickel, anyway. And it wasn't hopeless resignation, either. As a rule, Nucor people are not quitters.

Why, then, would workers who had endured deep cuts in pay and who had every reason to fear for their futures reach out to share a laugh with a *manager* passing through their mill? Simple. No employee was being asked to carry more than his or her part of the burden.

You see, their department heads had taken pay cuts of up to 40 percent, and the general managers and other officers of the company were earning 50–60 percent less than we had made in preceding years. My own pay dropped that year to about $110,000, from about $450,000 the year before. We not only *shared* the pain, we doled out the lion's share to the people at the top.

When a friend showed me an article, later that year, that listed me as the lowest-paid Fortune 500 CEO, I wasn't ashamed. The company was not performing. I'd have been ashamed to earn more.

—■-■-■—

"PAINSHARING" HAS HELPED us get through the tough times without ever laying off a single employee or closing a single facility for lack of work, even when the industry overall was shedding thousands of jobs. But our history of no layoffs is not noble, altruistic, or paternalistic. It's not even a company policy. We've told our employees time and again, "Nothing's written in stone. We'll lay people off if it is a matter of survival."

The question is, when is laying people off the practical and sensible thing to do? To compete over the long term, a company needs loyal, motivated employees. Can management expect employees to be loyal and motivated if we lay them off at every dip of the economy, while we go on padding our own pockets?

That last question sounds rhetorical, but it is not. Today's trend is still to compensate top management with huge sums that increase every year and bear no relation to how well or poorly the company and its workers are doing. I recently came across this *Wall Street Journal* headline: "Bethlehem Steel CEO Gets Pay Raise of 37% Despite Profit Drop." The article goes on to report that Bethlehem posted a loss of $309 million for the year. Net income was down 59 percent (not counting restructuring charges). The stock price fell 36 percent.[1] So tell me, how does the chief executive, who had been at the helm four years, justify a 37 percent increase in pay?

I admit, I like to gadfly the Big Steel companies, but there are plenty of other examples I could cite. Robert Allen of AT&T has earned millions while his corporation aborted its disastrous foray into the computer business and while thousands of the people who worked for him lost their jobs. I don't know the ins and outs of what happened there but, on its face, that's hard for me to accept. Banks are merging like crazy, and every merger or acquisition is followed by a bloodletting—except at the top, where executives either get promotions or ride off into the sunset, their saddlebags stuffed full of money. No wonder there is so much cynicism in the workplace!

We don't have much cynicism around Nucor. What's more, things have really changed since those dark days of 1982. We have prospered in an industry where many others have struggled. So we're not just unusual in terms of the commitment we've made to our people. We're unusually successful, too.

That's probably why you find so many journalists and business school professors poking around our company. They figure there's some kind of secret in there—some key to unlock the vault of happiness for the dispirited masses of corporate America, and some formula to bring out more of people's true productive potential.

In a sense, they're right. There is a key. A fellow named Ted Kuster from a publication called *New Steel* probably came closest to putting his finger on it. He wrote: "What Nucor management has been able to do is get workers to identify their own interests fundamentally with those of management, something managers have been attempting to do, not very successfully, since the dawn of industry."[2]

Kuster correctly identified the key: common interests. But he was wrong about one thing—Management didn't "get workers to identify" their interests with ours. That makes it sound like we tricked or manipulated employees into pushing their interests aside. We didn't.

What we did was push aside the notion that managers and employees have inherently separate interests. We've joined with our employees to pursue a goal we can *all* believe in: long-term survival. We run Nucor first and foremost to ensure that, a decade or two from now, there will still be a place for our children and grandchildren to work without being laid off. That is our higher cause.

Don't get the wrong idea—we each have our individual ambitions, too. Our employees want to make the very best living they can. And our executives worry about profitability as much as those in any company. We're people, not zealots.

But we're people with a long-term perspective. The way we see it, making a living in today's economy is like crossing a broad and stormy sea. You *could* jump straight in and start swimming. Of course, that would be foolish. People with sense will get together and build themselves a boat. And when the seas get a little rough, you could run around pushing your shipmates overboard. People with composure work together to pull through the storms. They deal with the perils of the moment together, never forgetting that the people around them represent their best hope of reaching a better future.

—■■■—

MANAGING WITH A long-term perspective is just common sense to us. But, I'll admit, not everybody sees things as we do. And, like managers in most large businesses, we must sometimes answer to those who froth at the mouth, pound on tables, and yell at us to do whatever it takes to maximize earnings *right now!* I'm referring, of course, to stock analysts.

Some of our officers recently met with a group of stock analysts in New York City. Here is the gist of my opening remarks to them:

Many of you, with your short-term view of corporations, remind me of a guy on drugs. You want that quick fix, that high you get from a big spike in earnings. So you push us to take on more debt, capitalize start-up costs and interest, and slow down depreciation and write-offs. All you're thinking about is the short term. You don't want to think about the pain of withdrawal that our company will face later on if we do what you want. Well, Nucor isn't going to respond to that kind of thinking. We never have and we never will.

These days, you can't swing a dead cat without hitting some corporate executive whining that Wall Street won't let him run the company for long-term growth. But I say complaining is a waste of time. In the end, you have to choose your master—the investor or the speculator.

What's the difference? Time. Over a three-to-five-year period, the success and growth in equity of a business will be reflected in its stock price, rewarding the investor. I've received letters from shareholders who assured us they won't cut and run should our earnings dip or our share price drop. "Do what's right," they say. "Keep the company strong. We're counting on you." One of my favorite letters came from a retired lady who had spent her career running a carpet store with her husband and making regular investments in Nucor stock. "I just wanted you to know," the letter said, "my husband has passed away, but I'm living very comfortably in Florida on the proceeds of our investment in your company." She believed in the system!

Speculators, of course, believe in the fast buck. They wave the capital in your face and expect you to abandon common sense. The amazing thing is, it works! Time and again, executives dance to their tune.

We refuse to do it. I like to remind our managers: "We're not dogs on a leash, doing tricks to manage the stock price or maximize dividends quarter-by-quarter. We're eagles. We *soar.* If investors want to soar, too, they'll invest in us. The speculators, we don't need."

———

EVERY DECISION WE make as managers is rooted in long-term perspective. You have to understand that in order to take in the true meaning of what I want to tell you about management.

A focus on long-term survival over shorter-term considerations can change every aspect of your business, because it drives fundamentally different priorities. Most of all, it is a safeguard against management's tendency to make business decisions solely in response to the pressures of the moment.

Nucor is now America's third-largest steel company. In 1996, our annual sales were more than $3.6 billion and our net income more than $248 million. Return on Equity has averaged better than 20 percent from 1990–1995.

If, during the bad times, we had failed to look past the short-term consideration of *this* quarter's earnings, would we have gone on to compile such a record of sustained growth and profitability? I'm certain we would not. If management had thought of our employees as nothing but "headcount"—a term that seems far more appropriate to cattle than to people—would they be as motivated and productive as they are today? Again, the answer is clearly no.

Many of our employees remember 1982 . . . the weight we bore together, and what management did when our backs were against the wall. We chose to save our company by working *with* employees, and they responded in kind.

When a journalist asked an employee at the Nucor Steel mill in Hickman, Arkansas why Nucor has no unions, he replied: "They're just not needed. The pay is top-notch. No one has been fired without cause. There are no layoffs. Nucor listens to its employees. We don't need union mediators. We don't need divisiveness. We all work together. We can talk among ourselves and work out our own problems."[3]

I ask our managers to focus, day in and day out, on maintaining close bonds with employees, because I believe people are our company's most valuable resource.

If you just chuckled to yourself, I don't blame you. Many executives say those words and few mean it. I can't help that. But I am sincere and so are our managers.

Our relations with employees are based on these four clear-cut principles:

1. *Management is obligated to manage the company in such a way that employees will have the opportunity to earn according to their productivity;*

2. *Employees should feel confident that if they do their jobs properly, they will have a job tomorrow;*

3. *Employees have the right to be treated fairly and must believe that they will be;*

4. *Employees must have an avenue of appeal when they believe they are being treated unfairly.*

We've found these are the fundamental things employees want and expect from our company. I imagine employees in any business would have similar expectations. And if you stop and think about it, they're not asking for much. Yet look at what employees typically get in corporate America.

Most don't get job security. Workers' short-term interests tend to run a distant third behind those of shareholders and executives. When those short-term interests conflict, people lose their jobs, no matter how hard they've worked (and no matter how much the company may need them down the line). That is why, through the longest economic expansion in history, many people remain haunted by the specter of recession and by memories of massive, dispassionate "reductions in force." And that is why so many workers remain deeply distrustful of management, even when managers try to rebuild the bridges of trust. After all, it was managers who tore down those bridges in the first place.

Employees know that their employers are generally determined to pay them as little as possible, however much they produce, and however much their labors earn for the company. Compensation reviews often surround employees in a smoke screen of "benchmark data," ambiguous goals, and subjective criteria. To some, it must seem as if the whole crazy system was cooked up to convince them that they are not as good as they think they are, and that they don't deserve what they think they deserve.

We have no performance appraisals in Nucor. People earn according to what they produce, and those earnings are determined simply and objectively. We also have no job descriptions. We let our employees define their own jobs as they search for ways to optimize their productivity.

What of employees' right to be treated fairly? Well, it's pretty hard to treat someone fairly when you view them as inherently unequal. Across corporate America, managers look down on the people they manage, and they distance themselves from employees with layer upon layer of hierarchy and management privileges.

Managers are supposed to do what's best for the business. And what's best is to remember we're all just people. Managers don't need or deserve special treatment. We're not more important than other employees. And we aren't better than anyone else. We just have a different job to do.

Mainly, that job is to help the people you manage to accomplish extraordinary things. That begins with remembering who does the *real* work of the business (something managers, with their outsized egos, often forget). It means relying on employees to make important decisions and take significant risks. And it means shaping a work environment that stimulates people to explore their own potential.

In these pages, I'll explain how and why I've tried to do those things throughout my career as a manager.

—◼◼◼—

AT NUCOR, people get what they *ought* to get from their work: Good pay. Real job security. Interesting challenges. Respectful treatment. The chance to accomplish something every day. A fair and equitable workplace. The pride of being a part of a very successful enterprise.

Nucor is no Shangri-la. But talk with people anywhere in our company and most of them will tell you, "Yes, I get all those things from my job." How many multibillion-dollar corporations can you say that about?

I hold Nucor up not as an ideal model to be emulated in every detail, but as proof that there are many ways to manage successfully. Our way is to look past the selfish and short-term interests that can divide the people of a business. We focus on the mutual, long-term interests that can unite us. We share a higher cause.

We don't think Nucor is better than other companies and we don't think Nucor people are different from other people. In fact, that's why we're compelled to explain how we do things, and why. We realize that most people out there, working for a living, are a lot like us. They want the same things we want. They want many of the things that we *have*. This book is our way of trying to share them.

2

TRUST YOUR INSTINCTS

IMAGINE THIS. . . . A corporation hands you complete control of a multimillion-dollar business operation. Then, as they send you off to run that business, they give you just three words of direction: "Trust your instincts."

That's pretty much what we do with the general managers who run our divisions.

Each division operates its one or two plants as an independent enterprise. They procure their own raw materials; craft their own marketing strategies; find their own customers; set their own production quotas; hire, train, and manage their own work force; create and administer their own safety programs. . . .

In short, all the important decisions are made right there at the division. And the general manager of the division is accountable for those decisions. That's where the buck stops at Nucor.

Not every manager is comfortable with that kind of latitude. In fact, it scares most of them half to death.

It probably should. In the mid-1970s, our general manager in Darlington, South Carolina, was determined to expand his facility using induction-melting furnaces rather than the arc furnaces our mini-mills normally used to melt down scrap metal. He had some pretty good reasons for wanting to go that way. Of course, others around Nucor jumped into the discussion with some pretty good reasons *not* to. There was no right or wrong answer. It came down to his instincts. The manager on the spot said, "I want the furnaces." So he got them. Cost us about $10 million.

Those furnaces gave our folks in Darlington fits. The main problem was the furnace linings. They wore out much more quickly than any of us expected. Shutting down time after time to replace the linings crippled production. This went on for a year or more.

The general manager who'd pushed to use induction furnaces left Nucor (for reasons that had nothing to do with the difficulties his mill was experiencing), and another general manager took over in Darlington. Some people around Nucor argued strongly for him to keep trying to make the furnaces work, and some argued just as vehemently that he should give up on them. Once again, though, the decision ultimately belonged to the manager on the spot. He called to tell me he was going to rip out our $10 million investment and put in standard arc furnaces. I told him I thought it was a good decision. There was no sense leaving the corpse lying around.

It must have been a tough call for him to make. But he didn't ask anyone to make it for him. That autonomy, that acceptance of decision-making responsibility *and* accountability, is something the people in our company refuse to live without. So we live with it, good and bad.

"We are honest-to-god autonomous," says Hamilton Lott, general manager of our Vulcraft Division in Florence, South Carolina. "That means that we duplicate efforts made in other parts of Nucor. The company might develop the same computer program six times. But, the advantages of local autonomy are so great, we think it's worth it."

"The beautiful part of Nucor is that we're not constrained," adds Joe Rutkowski, the current general manager of Nucor Steel in Darlington. "Headquarters doesn't restrict what I spend. I just have to make my contribution to profits at the end of the year."

Nucor has consistently required its general managers to generate a return of at least 25 percent on the assets we place under their control. The assets belong to the shareholders of the company, and entrusting them to a general manager is like making a deposit at the bank. The shareholders have every right to expect a healthy return.

"That's fine by me," Joe stresses. "I take the same approach with the people who work here in the division. My department heads, the people in the control rooms . . . they all spend thousands of dollars without anybody's approval. All of us can make that kind of decision, because all of us stand *behind* our decisions. We're accountable for getting the job done."

Beyond the minimum 25 percent return on assets employed, we require our general managers to abide by the ethical standards of the company and to follow a few general policies set down, as a group, by the general managers themselves. That's it. All the other decisions are left to the managers and employees of each division.

—■ ■ ■—

A LOT OF MANAGERS who want decision-making autonomy don't fully understand the responsibilities that come with that freedom. You have to accept that your operations will stand or fall on their own merits. There's no cavalry waiting to ride in to the rescue, and no mega-corporation in which to hide. There's just you and those people working with you.

Together, you'll find a way to succeed. Or you'll fail. So you'd better not forget how much is riding on your ability to communicate with employees.

That's the main reason we've tried to keep our divisions small. When a business grows beyond 400 or 500 people, it's hard for management and employees to stay connected.

I don't order our managers to keep in close contact with their employees. But I do nag them. I say, "Andrew Carnegie was a financier. He could afford to treat people like peasants. We're managers. We can't." They may not appreciate my nagging, but I do it with their interests in mind.

Different Nucor managers connect with their people in different ways. There's no cookie-cutter rule for how we want general managers to work with their people. Some meet with their department heads every morning. Others just once a quarter. Some spend more time walking the line than others. But they all stay connected in one way or another—or they don't last long.

I can't recall Nucor ever firing a general manager for not knowing how to make steel. But we have seen general managers fail to effectively lead people to the ambitious goals we set at Nucor. When that happens, we say "the employees fired the general manager." It's similar to when a football team loses faith in the coach. Who are you going to fire—the coach or the whole team?

We try to determine whether candidates for our manager positions will be able and willing to connect with their people. Department managers, for example, go through a screening process that has worked pretty well for us, including a standard psychological exam that identifies strengths and weaknesses in their skills. We don't want to put people into positions where they cannot succeed. We do want managers to be aware of how they may need to improve to make the grade with their people.

We once recruited an outstanding talent from outside the company to manage one of our divisions. This individual had an advanced degree in metallurgy *and* an M.B.A. He was brilliant. We were thrilled to have him.

But he was a complete dud as a manager. We smelled trouble when he surrounded himself with lieutenants whose primary function was to act as a buffer between him and the people who worked for him. You just can't do that in a small business. Some of us suggested to him that this wasn't a wise move . . . that we'd found it was essential to be in touch with the people around us . . . that a manager's authority comes *from* the employees. Distance yourself from your people and you distance yourself from your base of authority.

I've practiced what I've preached. Whenever I've run a plant, I've made it a practice to get around and talk with every manager in the plant each morning.

I'd sit and chat and drink coffee with people all over the facility. I might not get back to my own office and my own pile of work until late in the morning, and I'd arrive there with my caffeine quota for the day.

But it was always worth it. During my morning stroll, I might talk with a dozen or more people. I'd get an up-to-the-minute picture of what was going on in each and every part of the operation. Even more, I'd find out if people were feeling confident or anxious; see first-hand how well our technology was working; and get a sense which managers were struggling and which might be ready to take on more responsibility.

This was also a good way to get people used to seeing me, so I wouldn't scare them when the day came (as it surely would) that I needed information from somebody honestly and quickly.

By taking those strolls, I always knew what people thought. I had a strong sense of who they were, what they could do, and what they cared about. They knew the same things about me. I can't imagine staking my success on a group of people and *not* knowing them. It would be like trying to fly a plane with one wing.

Of course, there's more to staying in touch than getting out to talk informally with the people you manage. I'm also a big believer in conducting formal employee surveys. I've heard some business leaders say, "We don't need a survey. We talk to our people every day." Are they kidding? First of all, a survey is anonymous. Second, you're forcing people to stop and think about how they see things. If you take the survey results seriously, you also force *yourself* to stop and pay attention.

Every three years, Nucor surveys all employees. Our survey is nothing elaborate. It asks the usual questions about job satisfaction and takes the usual measures of organizational climate. But it is an important tool for staying connected.

One survey question asks each employee to tell us: "If you could change just one thing about Nucor, what would it be?" Some people write just a line or two. Others fill two or three pages. I try to read every single answer. We're under no obligation to do what employees suggest. But we are obligated to hear their point of view and to give it serious consideration. We do just that within each division and, during the years we conduct surveys, at our general managers' meetings. I believe it is among the most important things we do.

Some pretty big changes have come out of our survey process, like random drug testing. I was always against setting up drug screens. I thought it would be like telling our people "We don't trust you." But when more than 70 percent of our employees answered "Yes" to the question—"Should the company do random drug testing?"—we knew it was our duty to institute it. I still don't like it, but I can't argue with the logic. People's safety is at stake.

Each Nucor division has implemented random drug testing in its own way. Most of the joist plants require an employee who tests positive for drugs to enter a rehab program. A repeat offender is subject to termination. In most of the steel mills, though, the policy is "one strike and you're out," because a steel mill is just too dangerous a place to tolerate anyone working under the influence of drugs, even one time. The policy at most of our steel mills is: "If you test positive, you're fired." For someone who has worked hard at a job for fifteen or twenty years, that is a sudden and terrible thing. But the policy came from the people of Nucor. It is important to them. So it has to apply to everyone.

On the plus side, I've had employees come up to me and say: "You know, I used to mess around some with drugs. But I stopped. There's no way it was worth risking my job for." That makes me feel great.

Another change to come out of our employee survey was getting rid of time clocks. I liked that idea right from the start. Time clocks served no purpose. Our divisions are small enough that we know who's there and who isn't. And people didn't like being asked to punch in and punch out. So we got rid of the clocks. Would we have taken that step if we hadn't bothered to conduct the survey? I doubt it.

Sometimes we've tried ideas that came up in the survey, only to find they didn't work. One year, for example, we had quite a few requests for more options in our health plan. We made that change but, with health care costs skyrocketing, we soon found that our costs were getting out of hand. We were heading to a point where we'd be trading coverage for convenience. So we backed away from it. That was the right thing to do, too.

We provide a complete and straightforward report on the survey results back to employees, including the negative comments. In fact, we dedicate an entire issue of our quarterly newsletter to reporting our findings. But that's *all* we try to do at that time. Some managers seem to feel the need to answer every question and resolve every issue right away. But we think that's a mistake. First, if your survey is asking questions that really matter, there's no way you can come up with all the answers on the spot. Second, people need time to think about the problem for themselves before they're ready to consider whether or not the solution you offer is a good one.

The bottom line is, you don't want to turn survey results into some kind of quick-fix checklist for management. If you conduct the surveys regularly, study the results, share them with the company, and talk about them thoughtfully with others, it will show in your management decisions.

Employee meetings are another well-known way for managers to stay in touch with employees. But, as with employee surveys, not all companies use employee meetings to good effect.

Our employee meetings started in a few divisions in the late 1960s and early 1970s. They developed first into a tradition, then into a policy. We now ask our general managers to meet with all of their divisions' employees—in groups of no more than fifty—at least once each year. For a plant with 500 employees, that translates into at least ten employee meetings per year for the general manager. We require each general manager to give us the schedule of their meetings with employees.

Every division does the employee meetings a little differently. Some invite spouses, for example, while others are just for the people who work at the division. But all our employee meetings share certain fundamental characteristics that we've found, over the years, to be essential in making such meetings an effective way to stay connected.

First, the managers don't talk too much. If you pull employees together merely to serve as your audience, or to force them into participating in some kind of pep rally for the business, you're not going to connect with them. You'll push them away. At our employee meetings, the general manager of the division kicks off the discussion with comments that last no more than 20 minutes. Then, the employees take over. They talk about their equipment, rules and procedures, and anything else that pertains to how they see the business. Management listens.

Second, management takes what employees tell them seriously. Most employees have to screw up a bit of courage to stand up and present a real problem or issue to their managers. If management then just pays the issue lip service, the connection will be lost.

I went to a Vulcraft shift's meeting some years ago, and an employee stood up and said: "We're getting robbed blind out in the parking lot. They broke into my car and took my radio." Another stood up and said, "They siphoned out my gas!" Still another said, "Yeah, well they got my tires!"

Clearly, we had a problem although, before that night, management had not been aware of it. Now it was, thanks to the employee meeting. In exactly three days, that parking lot was fenced and fully lit.

Talking informally with your employees, conducting surveys, and organizing employee meetings are just three methods for connecting with the people who work for you. In fact, they're among the most common methods. What makes them valuable is not the methods themselves but the intent behind them. So, my advice boils down to this: If you want to manage autonomously, you'd better stay connected with your people, and if you want to stay connected with your people, you'd better be ready to give it an honest and sustained effort.

—■ ■ ■—

AN OLD ADAGE in business states that your degree of freedom is directly proportional to your distance from the corporate headquarters. None of our divisions are in the same town as our Charlotte, North Carolina headquarters. If any of them were, us headquarters types would always be over there, making suggestions and wasting their time with our opinions. A general manager running a division in Charlotte would feel like he was living with his mother-in-law.

We don't look over the shoulders of our general managers and we don't ask them to submit voluminous reports, explaining their actions. But that doesn't mean we're not paying attention. Delegation without information is suicide.

Every week, each division sends headquarters a few key numbers that, taken together, give us a "snapshot" of their basic operations from beginning to end:

- Quotes (bids)

- Orders

- Production

- Backlog

- Inventory

- Shipments

These numbers for all of Nucor's divisions print out on *one* 8.5″ × 11″ sheet of paper.

A second weekly report, about four pages long, compares the current week's numbers with those of the preceding week, shows each division's numbers over a period of thirteen weeks, and compares the current figures to the corresponding thirteen weeks of the preceding year. This enables us to look at trends. And since the reports are compiled by a computer, these comparisons are very easy to generate.

In total, then, we rely on about five pages of data to keep abreast of the weekly operations of twenty-one divisions across a multibillion-dollar corporation. I review the weekly reports every Wednesday morning over coffee. If the numbers for a particular division look out of whack, we know we need more information. John Correnti (Nucor's president and CEO) or I will call the general manager right away. They're rarely surprised to hear from us. They know when the numbers are likely to trigger questions. If, on the other hand, the numbers are on track, we assume their operations are doing just fine. We know they'll call us if they need us.

In short, while we work hard to get the information we need, we've worked just as hard to keep our reports streamlined and ourselves free of "information overload."

A lot of managers seem to miss the link between information overload and their compulsion to over-control their operations. But the connection is really obvious. Too much information puts you in the same position as too little information—you don't know what's going on. And when you don't know what's going on, it is hard to stay out of your people's hair. It's hard to tell them "trust your instincts," and really mean it.

Fighting off information overload hasn't been easy. When I was with Coast Metals in the early 1960s, our office got computers and I was inundated with data. I distinctly remember people coming in with thick stacks of computer printouts and dropping them on my desk. I went along with it at first. "The computer gave it to me, so it must be important," I reasoned. But it didn't take me long to figure out that a lot of the stuff a computer spits out at you is just plain useless.

You can't wait for someone else to come along and relieve you of the burden of information overload. You have to do it for yourself. You have to fight back. The key is to identify the fraction of information that truly is useful to *you*, so you can concentrate on it. That was how I gradually pared down the information I'd allow others to burden me with to the handful of data points I've just described.

I'd suggest that you try to focus on information that tells you what you need to know under ordinary circumstances, and that will give you early warning when something extraordinary is going on. If you experience a precipitous drop in orders, for example, you want to know immediately, so you can find out why and figure out what to do about it.

You should also take care to differentiate between *objective* and *subjective* information. A big part of information overload comes in the form of unneeded explanation (subjective information). I like to let the numbers do the talking, and decide for myself when they're not telling me all I need to know.

Look for information that documents cause-and-effect. You should be able to see a clear link between what's happening inside the operations you manage and what comes out in the way of business results. At Nucor, for example, we receive a somewhat more detailed report from each division at the end of each month. This report, like those we receive weekly, is all data and no text. It updates us on each division's costs against budgets, sales revenue, monthly contribution to earnings, and monthly return on assets employed. In other words, it shows us the *results* the division has generated for the month from the *operations* we've tracked weekly. Putting together the weekly and monthly reports shows us cause and effect. It is also simple to understand.

Finally, I'd suggest you focus on information that is easy for others to provide, so your information needs won't take away from their real work, and so you can rely on them to provide the information you need consistently.

When you gather truly useful information efficiently and consistently, you'll know what's going on. And when you know what's going on, you'll find it's a lot easier to let your people trust their instincts.

————■■■————

WE GIVE OUR managers and employees so much autonomy, some have painted me as a "champion of decentralization." Nucor *is* decentralized, of course. But I'm no zealot. I can imagine building a successful company on a centralized model. It would be a very different company, of course. It might also be more difficult to manage. But it could be a successful company, nevertheless.

I served on the board of directors for Wal-Mart, and you won't find many more centralized operations. As I recall, even the temperature of Wal-Mart stores was controlled from Wal-Mart's headquarters in Bentonville, Arkansas. Now *that's* centralization. And centralization certainly hasn't stopped Wal-Mart from compiling an astounding record of profitable business growth.

My point is: Decentralization isn't "good." Centralization isn't "bad." Each is a sound option under the right circumstances.

Businesses that need to operate uniformly wherever they are—McDonald's or Wal-Mart, for example—must be shaped by relatively few people. In such a business, centralized decision making is a very sensible approach.

Businesses that serve diverse markets, on the other hand—or that experience very different conditions in different locations, or that rely more on high levels of innovation and flexibility than on uniformity—are best shaped by a wider array of people. . . . That is, by the people closest to where the work actually gets done. Those businesses must tell people on the front lines to "trust your instincts." And businesses that tell their people to "trust your instincts" generally should be decentralized. A decentralized structure pushes the power to set strategy, spend money, make decisions, and create policies out toward the marketplace. It promotes local autonomy.

Managers within companies can look at the operations for which they are accountable in much the same way. In your department or work group, what's more important, uniformity or innovation? Consistency or flexibility? If your success depends heavily on uniformity and consistency, centralized decision making may be justified. If your success relies more on innovation and flexibility, you should make a conscious effort to push decision-making power down.

An awful lot of companies can't seem to make up their minds about whether they want decision making to be centralized or decentralized. First, they break up operations and decision-making authority and disperse them to the field. They set up "small business units," talk about "getting close to the customer," and strive to "empower" front-line employees who need more autonomy and (as a result) more flexibility to do their jobs well. I imagine most achieve some measure of success in these efforts. That is, until HQ pulls the power back in, usually as a cost-cutting tactic aimed at "eliminating redundancies."

And so it goes, like an accordion expanding and contracting, with all those people getting squeezed inside. Each swing from centralized decision making to local autonomy and back to centralization may bring layoffs, restructuring, and other disruptions to the business, not to mention a growing sense among employees that management is (at best) confused.

The only two reasons I can think of to take a business through such a gut-wrenching transition are: *a*) to change what business you are in, or *b*) to respond to truly fundamental changes in your business environment. Cost-cutting, efficiency, and cycle-time reduction are *not*, in my view, valid reasons to centralize or decentralize a business. You can pursue those goals under either construct.

So, you see, I'm not so much a champion of decentralization as I am an advocate for decisiveness. Managers at all levels need to assess what is most crucial for the operations they manage and—based on that assessment—choose where the locus of decision-making power should reside. Then they must implement that choice thoroughly, and stick to their choice over the long term. Whichever way you choose, you give up something. But by failing to choose, you can give up everything.

—▪▪▪—

Companies that choose to decentralize and to spread decision making and accountability around must take steps to maintain some level of unity within their operations.

The greatest counterweight to divisiveness in Nucor is that the general managers of our divisions are also officers of our corporation. Most of the year, a general manager is preoccupied with running his own show. He thinks about his own revenue totals, his own profits, and his own return on assets employed. But three times each year—in November, February, and May—he takes off his general manager's hat to focus on his role as an officer of the corporation. He meets with the other general managers to set policies and make decisions that shape Nucor, as a whole.

These meetings usually begin with a 3- to 4-hour session on a Wednesday evening, then run all day Thursday and Friday and, occasionally, into the weekend.

In November, the general managers present budgets for their divisions for the upcoming year. They also outline their plans for capital expenditures.

In February, we finalize the budgets and capital plans.

The May meeting is devoted almost entirely to human resource issues, compensation, safety, and benefits. Collectively, the general managers created our personnel policies, and they refine them each May.

The meetings belong to the general managers. We don't subject them to mind-numbing presentations from headquarters types. In fact, just a handful of us from HQ participate. When you bring together managers who spend most of their time acting autonomously—people you've told to "trust your instincts"—the last thing you want to do is tell them to sit still and listen.

"At those meetings, there's very little of the Charlotte headquarters people talking at us. It's mostly us talking to them, and to each other," says Joe Rutkowski, general manager of Nucor Steel in Darlington. "We talk about what's important to *us*."

There's a healthy tension to these meetings, too. People yell. They wave their arms around and pound on tables. Faces get red and veins bulge out. A new general manager in his first meeting might hold his tongue. But that doesn't last long. "A year or two of running our own show turns us all into experts," Joe Rutkowski notes.

Put that many confident, headstrong personalities in a room together and sparks are bound to fly. I think that's a good thing. In fact, I worry when the sparks *don't* fly. These meetings are designed to let each of us tap into the collective wisdom of all of us. That wisdom won't come out if we're worried about stepping on one another's toes. The business can't afford that. We're there to talk about issues that are important. Very important. And very important issues can be sensitive. So be it.

Many years ago, when I was working in a foundry up in Muskegon, Michigan, I got pretty ticked off about something someone had said. The president of the company grabbed hold of my arm, the way some older guys will when demanding the attention of a younger man, and said to me: "Remember, Ken, a good manager has to be hard to bruise and quick to heal." That was a good lesson, one I've passed on to many other managers. You can't be too quick to take offense.

There are some boundaries for what's acceptable in the general managers' meetings, of course, and I'm often the one who points them out. I take into account that these are people with big egos. We're all *for* big egos. But we're against building up your ego by stepping on the back of someone else. As a firm rule, we don't discuss personalities. If I see that happening, I step in and put a stop to it as quick as I can.

Most everything else is fair game. Our general managers say what they think, even if they know I won't like it. (They do that quite a lot, in fact.)

Motive is the key. It's a heck of a lot easier to listen to someone tear down your position when you know the disagreement is honest, objective, and motivated by what they truly believe is good for the company. That's what makes it possible for managers to disagree, to argue, and to criticize, then resolve the issue and move on. Our general managers are very good at that.

These gatherings remind our general managers that their idea isn't the only idea, and that their answer isn't the only answer. They do that for each other three times a year. They may not always like it, but they know it's healthy. When you have power, *real* power, as Nucor's general managers do, you need to stay humble.

You also need to be circumspect. General managers run their own businesses. They call their own shots. But they have to hold up their plans, decisions, *and* their results to the scrutiny of their peers. That's a very effective check against making impulsive decisions, whether it's a multimillion-dollar capital investment or a key promotion.

Many times, a general manager will say something like, "I've got the best rolling manager in the company. I'm going to promote him and give him a big raise." Then the other general managers produce numbers to demonstrate that this particular rolling manager's performance has actually fallen behind that of his counterparts in other divisions. The general manager stops and thinks, "Maybe my rolling manager's not as good as I think he is." The opposite occurs nearly as often. General managers learn to appreciate just how good certain individuals are when they see how their performance compares with that of others, and when other general managers hold those individuals in high esteem.

Open debate also safeguards against little problems getting tucked away in some dark corner, where they can grow into big problems. If one general manager has a beef with another, it's bound to find its way onto the table during the course of a meeting. That's where we want them, out in the light of day, so we can nip them in the bud.

By bringing these natural rivals together to debate, to resolve issues, to set policies, and to collectively make decisions, we make Nucor one company, even as each division stands mostly on its own. It's a way to retain an emotional bond. Caring enough to really take issue with someone's idea is, in the end, a demonstration of support. We try to keep each other from screwing up. You can't stay mad at someone for doing that.

The fundamental principles that shape how we run all of Nucor grew out of our general managers' meetings. Our policies and strategies are a product of that open exchange of ideas and perspectives. I've listened to those general managers talk about nearly everything, and what they've said has impressed me.

I can't tell you how many times I've heard a Nucor general manager say that "this is how we ought to structure compensation" or "this is how we should look at risks," and thought: "Yeah, that's the right way to run a business." I've latched onto those ideas and pushed them around Nucor as hard as I can. Some people assume they are all *my* ideas. I should be so smart.

—■■■—

I'VE READ BOOKS by management experts who say, "A good manager is a good manager in any kind of business. He can go anywhere and succeed." Don't believe it. Good management is situational. There's no guarantee that a great manager in a retail environment, for example, will be a great manager in construction. Experience in the business is a huge advantage. In fact, it is often essential. And the fundamental approaches that prove effective in one business can easily fail you in the next.

But while there are many good ways to manage, there is no excuse for being wishy-washy about how *you* will manage. You must *choose*—Where will decisions be made, and by whom, within your operations?

At Nucor, we chose long ago to build our company on a decentralized model in which each operating division enjoys true autonomy. We have told our managers to "trust your instincts"—and we have meant what we said. We've urged them to confer the same kind of decision-making autonomy to their people—to make their own decisions based on what *they* think is best for the business—and we have never backed off our commitment.

Before making your choices, you must think through which decision-making structures will best serve the operations you manage.

We chose decentralization to gain the innovation, speed, and flexibility that stem from operating like twenty-one smaller companies instead of as a monolithic corporation. We're willing to live with the redundancies and "inefficiencies" that go with that choice.

After you choose, you must live up to the obligations inherent in your choices. Under a decentralized structure that urges people to "trust your instincts," those obligations include making an honest and sustained effort to stay connected with your people, shielding yourself from information overload, and engaging in open, constructive debate. That's a lot harder than handing out orders, but it is also a lot more interesting.

3

DESTROY THE HIERARCHY

I N 1962, just after I moved from New Jersey down to Florence, South Carolina, to manage Vulcraft, I received a phone call from the principal of a local high school. "Mr. Iverson," the principal inquired, "would you come over to Wilson High and say a few words to our students at assembly?" I said I'd be delighted and we chose the date.

"You're going out to *Wilson?!*" a neighbor gasped when I told him of the invitation. "Ken, did you know that Wilson is the Negroes' high school?" I confessed that I did not. "Oh, yeah," this fellow said knowingly. "They got themselves a nice new building, but I hear they've made a shambles of it already."

Well, I went out there and the school was immaculate. The principal greeted me with a smile that radiated pride, and the smile never left her face as she led me through the halls of Wilson High. The students filing into assembly were happy, energetic, orderly, and courteous. The teachers I met were professional and caring. In short, Wilson High was a place brimming with people who, like me, saw education as a precious gift, and who were doing everything within their considerable powers to make Wilson a fine school. I had a delightful time.

Driving back to Vulcraft, I thought about my neighbor, the one who had prepared me to expect the worst from Wilson High. He seemed a reasonably intelligent man, in touch with reality, and knowledgeable about the community. He was also a friendly sort and, so far as I could tell, had no particular ax to grind. How could he have been so wrong about the place?

The answer was clear. The notion that white society was superior to black society was so ingrained in this region, one didn't have to be stupid or delusional or mean to accept the status quo. It just *was*. In 1962, I attended a company Christmas party for whites and a company Christmas party for blacks. Blacks and whites used separate washrooms and drank from separate fountains. At a ceremony celebrating the completion of a new addition to our plant, a consultant who had set up the event asked me: "When do you want to have the Negroes come through?" The whole world, it seemed, had been divided up into "*We* vs. *They*." And the "We" just naturally assumed the worst in the "They," facts be darned.

This sad truth forced me to confront a dilemma, a *practical* dilemma, not a moral one. I didn't come to South Carolina to combat racism. I came to manage. I had a business to run, and I knew that to make Vulcraft perform the way I knew it could, I'd have to convince everyone to work together and to respect one another as equals.

This may surprise you as much as it surprised me, but the first real step in putting an end to all that "*We* vs. *They*" thinking turned out to be *listening*, although that wasn't my plan. I charged out in my usual way to talk one-on-one with each department head. But on my very first stop, the engineering manager politely but firmly set me straight. "Mr. Iverson," he said, "you're doing this all wrong. Don't burst into my office each morning at 10 a.m. and start talking business. Down here, we talk about other things first." Other things? "That's right," he explained. "We talk about my family, your family, football, the weather, the goings on around town . . . then, if there's time, we talk business. That's pretty much required for polite conversation."

That really gave me pause. He was trying to help me, I could see that. And I sure didn't want to offend people who held the key to Vulcraft's success, so I decided to try it his way, and see what happened.

It turned out to be a fine piece of advice. I'm sure most of the people I spoke with those first few days could see that it was a bit awkward for me, exchanging small town gossip or debating which team might win the high school football game on Friday night. But I was making an honest effort. They recognized that I was ready to adjust as best I could to what they considered important. That made it a heck of a lot easier for me to ask them to adjust, too, to something I thought was important. A week after I arrived, I knocked down the wall that separated the white employees' locker room from the locker room used by the blacks. I couldn't eliminate the barriers that separated people into "We" vs. "They" out in the rest of the world, but I could darn sure do it inside Vulcraft.

Inequality still runs rampant in most business corporations. I'm referring now to *hierarchical* inequality, which legitimizes and institutionalizes the principle of "We" vs. "They" in Corporate America, just as racial inequality was once legitimized and institutionalized in American society. Ivory tower office suites. Executive parking spaces. Employment contracts. Corporate jets. Limousines. Hunting lodges. First-class travel. Meetings at posh resorts. Company cars. Executive dining rooms. The people at the top of the corporate hierarchy grant themselves privilege after privilege, flaunt those privileges before the men and women who do the *real* work, then wonder why employees are unmoved by management's invocations to cut costs and boost profitability.

I'm often amazed at the lengths to which executives will go to separate themselves from the people they manage. In *Crisis in Bethlehem*, John Strohmeyer recounts that executives at Bethlehem Steel built themselves a beautiful golf course with corporate funds. There was some grumbling from the ranks, so they built a second course for middle managers, and eventually a third course for employees.[1] Imagine building *three* golf courses just to remind everyone where they fall in the corporate hierarchy! What does that say about a company's values and corporate culture?

It's helpful to think of corporate culture as all the things that shape interactions among the people in your company, its customers, and suppliers. The term that comes closest to describing Nucor's culture, I think, is "egalitarian."

America was founded on the idea that people are inherently equal, regardless of whether they're rich or poor, young or old, powerful or weak. So you could make a pretty good case for an egalitarian culture on ideological grounds alone. Yet there's no need for ideology. The best case for promoting equality rests on practical considerations like productivity, efficiency, profitability, and growth. A business needs motivated employees to compete over the long term, and an egalitarian business culture is an extraordinarily practical way to sustain employee motivation.

—■■■—

MANAGERS TEND TO see promoting equality or "empowering employees" as a product of their non-interference. Even I find myself counseling managers to "just stay out of the way" of their employees. But the truth is, you can't be passive. You must attack hierarchy. You have to destroy it.

I sensed an opportunity to do just that, a few years back, when I read an article in the *Wall Street Journal* about a Canadian company where everyone wore the same color hard hats. That intrigued me. In Nucor plants, like most hard hat environments, workers, supervisors, department managers, and the general manager of the facility all wore different color hard hats, signifying their place in the hierarchy. And a high-ranking executive visiting from headquarters might be given a gold hard hat to wear, as a symbol of his lofty status. This was in keeping with industry tradition, but it seemed so contrary to our goal of maintaining an egalitarian culture, I decided right then and there, without consulting anyone, that all Nucor personnel would wear green hard hats, and all visitors would wear white, from then on, no exceptions.

The phone didn't stop ringing for a week! I'll bet fifty supervisors called or wrote me to protest the move. "You can't do that!" they'd say. "That hat shows who I am. It makes me proud. I put it in the back window of my car when I drive home, so everyone knows I'm a Nucor supervisor. On the job, it's my badge of authority. Why are you taking it away?"

I could see their point, but it didn't seem a good enough reason to continue a practice that was so clearly inconsistent with our goal of an egalitarian culture. We ran a series of informal seminars for managers and supervisors at different Nucor facilities to help them make the adjustment. We worked hard to convince them that their authority and status didn't come from the color of their hat. It came from who they are and how they act and all they had accomplished. On balance, I'd say we gained grudging acceptance from most of them, and after a few months everybody was pretty comfortable with the new policy.

My hard hat policy did prove flawed in one significant respect, though. Maintenance people needed to be spotted quickly when there was a problem with equipment. In my haste to sweep away a symbol of hierarchy, I'd ignored this very sensible reason to have some people wear a different colored hard hat. One of my favorite sayings is, "Good managers make bad decisions." Forgetting to set apart maintenance people was a mistake. When it was pointed out to me, I admitted as much and agreed that the maintenance crews could wear yellow hats.

When Nucor acquired a bearing products plant about ten years ago, the first thing we did was sell off the limousine, the second was to get rid of the executive parking spaces. All it took was a little black paint. But talk about making people happy! As I stood outside the plant to meet some of our new employees, a young man stopped, smiled, and pointed back toward the lot, saying, "Look where I'm parked. That's the *boss's* spot."

"You mean, that *was* the boss's spot," I said.

"Yeah, I guess so," the young man said with a chuckle. Then he turned quite serious. "You know, that makes me feel a whole lot better about working here," he said.

Exactly. How do you think employees feel on a rainy day when they have to park clear across the lot, while right in front of the door are two or three spaces, waiting for some manager who is on a trip out of town? Employees want managers to stop acting like they're somehow better or more important than everyone else.

When I think of the millions of dollars spent by people at the top of the management hierarchy on efforts to motivate people who are continually put down *by* that hierarchy, I can only shake my head in wonder. What on earth are they thinking? We think you can get a heck of a lot further simply by minimizing the distinction between management and any other employee in the company.

Our executives get the same group insurance, same holidays, and same vacations as everybody else. They eat lunch in the same cafeterias. They fly economy class on regular commercial flights (although we do allow the use of frequent flyer upgrades). We have no executive suites and no executive cars. At headquarters, our "corporate dining room" is the deli across the street.

Our executives wouldn't have it any other way. They see our egalitarian culture serving their interests as much as the interests of our employees. For one thing, our managers don't have to waste time fretting over their chances to get the fancy corner office or arguing over who gets to use the company plane. We don't have those perks, and we imagine they would cause a lot more stress than fulfillment. What a bunch of nonsense! Chasing meaningless status symbols and tokens of power. When you look back on your career, will those things seem important?

—■-■-■—

MY LONGEST-RUNNING battle against hierarchy has been holding the line against more layers of management. Nucor—a $3.6 billion corporation—operates with just four management layers:

Chairman/President

General Managers

Department Managers

Supervisors/Professionals

Think of it . . . No one in the company is more than four promotions away from having my job! The typical Fortune 500 corporation, in contrast, has 8 to 12 layers of management.

When Nucor first approached $1 billion in revenues, more than a few people told me, "Now you *have* to add more layers of management." I refused. The same thing happened when we reached the $2 billion and $3 billion milestones.

First off, I never bought into the old "span of control" theories they taught managers back when I was starting out. They said that if you were managing six people, you needed another manager. That notion always seemed far too restrictive—yet another manifestation of management's tendency to underestimate the people who work for them. Some supervisors at Nucor directly manage forty or fifty people, and do it very well.

More to the point, I think adding more layers of management would wreck one of the great strengths of our business—very short lines of communication. "You can find out anything you want to know in a hurry," says Dan DiMicco, who manages the Nucor-Yamato Steel joint venture in Blytheville, Arkansas, "because you don't have to go through channels. You just pick up the phone or go see the person with the information you need. Most of the time, it's easy." Wouldn't most managers be thrilled to say that?

From where I sit, I know that if I have to communicate through a Group Vice President, a Regional Manager, and a District Manager, the message that comes out the other end won't sound much like what I said in the first place. Why should I take a step that will make it harder to get my messages across, clearly and intact?

The same goes for information people want to send *up* through the hierarchy. Now, some may argue that not every idea should find its way to the top levels of decision making, and I'd agree. But it is hard to picture *any* idea—no matter how wonderful—actually making it all the way up from an hourly employee through ten layers of management without it being fatally diluted or commandeered by a higher-up.

And executives wonder why employees are sometimes apathetic about suggestion systems! The reason is clear—far too many of the ideas that people offer lose momentum and die, like spawning salmon forced to scale too many waterfalls. If you asked me, the solution to this problem isn't, "Let's build a better suggestion system." It is "Let's get rid of some of the waterfalls!" Strip out a half-dozen or so layers of the management hierarchy, and employees' information and ideas will find their own way to wherever they need to go.

Of course, there are limits to the virtues of "destroying the hierarchy." You probably can't tear it out altogether, although I've heard of businesses that have experimented with that very idea. I've long been fascinated with W. L. Gore & Associates, the makers of Gore-Tex® fabrics. This privately held company has used a whole different management concept. As I understand it, the essence of that concept is: "There is no leader. The group is the business." Bill Gore told the story of when a young lady at the company was invited by a local association to make a speech on how Gore Associates was run. The group asked her to send them a business card and a title, but people at Gore Associates had neither. So Mr. Gore made up a little business card for her with the title "Supreme Commander."

I don't imagine a company the size of Nucor could run without some kind of management hierarchy, but I'm certain it can run with no more than four layers, and I'll be surprised if anyone convinces me that we truly need more. I've learned to stay alert to the signs of an expanding hierarchy: Cliques within divisions . . . Reams of memos . . . Conflicts between department managers . . . Committees . . . Communications bottlenecks . . . Non-stop meetings. Where hierarchy lurks, these evils will rear their ugly heads. I try my best to stamp them out. Our goal is to just let people go ahead and *do* things.

—■■■—

SINCE WE'VE FOUND that at least a minimal management hierarchy is necessary, I firmly believe that employees must have an avenue of appeal—a place they can turn to when they feel that management has not adequately or fairly responded to their concerns. At Nucor, the ultimate avenue of appeal is either me or Nucor's CEO, John Correnti. We've promised to hear any employee's point of view, to be as impartial as possible, and to provide a quick response.

Our company policy says that anyone in the company can write to us with a complaint. But that's not the way it usually works. Most of the time, people just pick up the phone and call us. Everyone knows they can call us directly because others who have done it tell them that it's okay. I try to answer my own phone whenever I can. I've never found it necessary to have someone screen my calls. If I don't pick up the phone myself, it's usually because I'm not there or because I'm already talking with someone else.

Employees who call may remain anonymous (although they almost always give their name), and there are no ground rules, formal or informal, for what they may call us about. Sometimes the callers have no substantive complaint. They just need to get something off their chest. They blow off a little steam and we're done. Most of the time, though, employees won't call unless they have a serious problem that they and their managers can't resolve.

I once received a call from an employee who'd been fired for leaving his plant without notifying his supervisor. For safety reasons, we need to know who is and who is not in the plant. But as I learned when he called me, this employee's son had been involved in an accident. When he got word of it, the man had rushed out of work to go to the hospital, forgetting to tell anyone. The supervisor who fired him was following the book at a time when common sense dictated we put the book aside. After I finished talking with the employee, I called the general manager of the division. We soon agreed that this was an exception to the rule. The employee kept his job.

Another employee had been fired for putting false figures in his production report. He was 23 years old, a new supervisor, trying hard to impress everyone. He called and asked to see me, so I told him to come on in. He drove all the way to Charlotte from Indiana and arrived in my office accompanied by his brother-in-law, who worked at the same plant and, it turns out, was the one who reported him for falsifying the figures. There was no question that what the young man had done was a serious transgression of business ethics. It was almost unforgivable. But I was convinced he knew that. I told him I'd look into his situation, then talked it over with his department manager and the general manager at that division. We decided it would be wrong to wreck a man's career and possibly his life for one mistake, even one so serious. He's still with the company and he's doing very well.

Believe me, I think long and hard before I overturn a standing rule or urge a manager to forgive an employee's dishonesty. And I don't do it very often. The main thing I think about in deciding how to respond to such situations is: "When everybody else in the company learns of it (as they surely will), will they believe we did the right thing?" If I suspect that our action will be seen as contradicting our basic values, I won't make an exception. If I think they'll see bending the rules as a demonstration of our caring for one another and as something that will be good for the company in the long term, I will.

The most difficult phone calls I've received come from employees who have tested positive for drugs and lost their jobs. Some have said to me: "I work hard. I'm an honest person. I *need* the job." And you know every word is true. That makes me feel awful. I want so badly to give them one more chance. But there is absolutely nothing I can do. That's one rule our people have asked us never to bend, because a coworker on drugs is too great a hazard in our work environments.

My objective during the call itself is to *listen* to the employee, not to resolve his problem. I find out what the facts are, get their side of the story, and take time to hear how they feel about it and *why* they feel the way they do. I think most managers and executives have a tendency to think they have to come up with a brilliant answer, Bing!, when what the caller really wants is simply to be heard. Being heard is liberating. It demonstrates to employees that they are not buried under layer after layer of bureaucracy. If an employee is concerned enough to bring a problem or issue to you, then you ought to listen. It's common courtesy and it's good for the business.

Between us, John and I receive an average of about four employee calls per month, and that's out of a total of nearly 7,000 employees. The low number of calls isn't because our people never have issues or problems. It's because we have good managers who listen to their people. I always ask a caller if he has discussed the problem with his supervisor, department manager, and general manager. If he has not, I urge him to try that path first, knowing he's likely to get a full and fair hearing. Our managers will try their best to work out a solution. That's their nature. Besides, they know that if they won't listen to their employees' problems, I will.

———■·■·■———

SHARING INFORMATION IS another key to treating people as equals, building trust, and destroying the hierarchy. I think there are really just two ways to go on the question of information-sharing: *Tell employees everything or tell them nothing*. Otherwise, each time you choose to withhold information, they have reason to think you're up to something. We prefer to tell employees everything. We hold back nothing.

"By sharing everything, we give our people the opportunity to do their jobs to the best of their ability," John Correnti, our CEO, has noted. "Employees need a lot of information to manage themselves and to keep our costs in line. Besides, our incentive pay is based on group productivity results.

"Obviously, some of the information we share flows to the street," John adds. "But the value of sharing everything with our employees is much greater than any downside there might be to some information getting out. It hasn't seemed to hurt us through 27 years of profitable growth in an industry that hasn't consistently done well."

Nucor Steel in Hickman, Arkansas, for example, recently instituted an adjustment to the production bonus through which employees earn income above and beyond their base wage. These adjustments are necessary, from time to time, to compensate for the investments the company makes in new technology which, in combination with the ingenuity of our employees, drives productivity (and production bonuses) to higher and higher levels.

Some Hickman employees questioned whether the bonus adjustment was justified and asked to see some comparative data. Mike Parrish, the general manager at Hickman, gathered data on production bonus levels throughout Nucor and published it in his "green sheet," a weekly bulletin to employees distributed by most Nucor general managers. Mike shared the bonus data even though he realized it could be read to support the arguments *against* adjusting the production bonus.

"If I were a production worker here, I'd want to see that data and I'd want the chance to state my point of view," Mike explains. "By sharing the data, we maintained trust, even if the numbers themselves didn't cause everyone to agree that the adjustment was warranted. Looking at those numbers, I still thought it was the right time to move the production baseline. I did my best to explain why. I listened to the employees who were concerned. They listened to me. Nobody was holding anything back. And that made it a little easier for them to accept a decision that is in the best interests of everyone, long-term.

"It also helps to have no executive perks to defend during a time like this," Mike adds. "I've got the same medical coverage as them. I buy my own car, just like they do. They don't see me as a guy trying to take their money to line my pockets. They know I'm trying to do what's best for the company, overall, and for everyone in it, not just for me."

—■■■—

OUR EGALITARIAN CULTURE is a big reason why our managers don't have to deal with unions or spend a lot of time thinking about how to keep unions out of our company, although our industry is overwhelmingly unionized. "Unions are basically just another layer of management," says Dan DiMicco. "All it does is add another filter for communications to pass through, and that's bound to make my life harder than it has to be."

For the most part, our employees don't seem to like unions much. They generally see unions as outsiders trying to push their way in and take a slice of their pie.

One day, five or six years ago, a union organizer positioned himself outside our mill in Darlington, South Carolina, to hand out pamphlets and talk to the workers who were arriving for their shift. That was the union man's right under the law and, as our policy is to obey the law, our managers ignored him.

A few workers stopped, though, to state that they didn't need any union's help. They strongly suggested that the organizer move on and find somebody who did. But the orgranizer stood his ground and continued to pitch his union.

When the circle of Nucor workers tightened around the union man, a couple of our managers hustled out to help him beat a hasty retreat to his car. He left ashen-faced, without a peep of protest, and headed down the road (at a good clip, I'm told) in search of friendlier hunting grounds.

I think some companies deserve unions. Their managers just don't treat employees right. They use the hierarchy to keep people down. But when a company's managers treat employees as equals, they earn trust. And the bond of trust enables managers to do things that would never fly in a company based on "*We* vs. *They*."

Take, for example, our practice of listing every Nucor employee, in alphabetical order, on the cover of our annual report. In a lot of companies, that would be seen (justifiably) as a hollow gesture. In ours, it's an expression of what we truly believe, that each and every one of those people is equally important. And let me tell you, if we mistakenly leave off a name, we hear about it from that employee, even though the print is getting so small some of us have to search for our names with a magnifying glass.

Mike Parrish hand-delivers a birthday card to each of his 350-plus employees. "It's a way to make sure I talk with everyone directly at least once each year, and by doing that I get a real good idea of what's happening all over the mill," he says. In most businesses, the head of a division delivering a birthday card to a crane operator in his cab would seem ludicrous, and many employees would react to such a gesture with a mix of suspicion and cynicism. But Mike gets the benefit of the doubt. This isn't a manager who rides around on a high horse most of the time, looking down at you. This is a colleague who's busy and who carries a lot of responsibility, yet cares enough to come out and find you and to talk with you and let you know he appreciates having you around, wherever you may work in the mill.

—■■■—

PURE EQUALITY BRINGS out pure adrenaline and pure effort. It is a beautiful sight and, as our people will tell you, an exhilarating experience. When hot steel breaks out of a caster in a Nucor mill, everyone in the vicinity—manager, supervisor, hourly employee— jumps into the fray. It's not chaotic, but you'd have a hard time telling who's the boss. People speak sharply to one another ("C'mon, get over here!" "Johnny, grab hold of the other end!") with no deference to one's rank in the management hierarchy. The tone is urgent, but controlled. Arguments are rare. When things get hot, you don't have time for conflict. You're too busy trying to get the job done. When the breakout has been brought under control, the most skilled electrician will matter-of-factly pick up a shovel or broom and help clear the area of debris, right along with everyone else.

Employees aren't perfect, but if you give them half a chance, they'll usually step up and do the right thing. My faith in the ethics and abilities of working people is rooted far back in my career.

Prior to taking a job with Vulcraft, I was the executive vice president of the Coast Metals foundry in Little Ferry, New Jersey, where we were making molded metal castings to go into aircraft. The workers in the machine shop there had posters of semi-nude girls on the walls, the kind you might see in automotive repair shops. The posters had been up for years, and we'd never had a complaint about them, but part of my job was to lead inspectors from our biggest customer, Pratt & Whitney, on tours of our facility, and I felt that those posters were inappropriate. So I asked the machine shop workers to take the posters down.

Well, they pitched a fit. "Those posters have always been there! Why do they have to come down now all of a sudden?!" I didn't blame them. The machine shop was their area. They didn't like me telling them to change it. I let them blow off steam for a while, then I explained my reasons for wanting the posters down. They saw, then, that I wasn't just trying to boss them around. So one of them asked, "How would it be if we moved the posters inside the tool lockers, where visitors won't see them?" That was fine with me. We solved the problem. Nobody had to back down, and nobody held any grudges.

The average employee in the United States is also a lot smarter than most managers will give him credit for. If you really want answers you can use to make the business perform better, ask the people who are doing the actual work of the business. It's that simple. Front-line employees continually amaze me with their capacity to make improvements.

The shipping crews at Nucor-Yamato, for example, found that the truck trailers the company was buying (at a cost of about $35,000 each) were not ideally suited to carry the huge I-beams we make there out of the plant to our railroad siding, tractor-trailer depot, and barge pier. So they designed and constructed their *own* trailers, using materials at hand to make everything but the wheel assemblies.

Dave Chase, our hot mill manager in Hickman, summed it up best when he told me, "People come to our mill and they see our equipment putting out these extraordinary numbers of tons per hour, and they say, 'I'm going to get us that equipment.' 'Good idea,' I tell them, 'but you ought to know, it's not the equipment turning out all that steel. It's the people.' "

People generally love the chance to seize initiative, to shape their own lives and to command their own destinies. So we try to provide those opportunities to the people who work in our office environments, as well. And it works. If a receptionist finds it hard to get her kids off to school and still be at her desk by 8 a.m., she turns first to her coworkers. Nine times out of ten, they'll find a way to cover for her or to solve whatever problem needs solving. Management rarely needs to get involved.

Ask people around Nucor why they choose to work for our company, and the word "freedom" comes up often. "We're the company. We control its destiny more than the senior managers do, in my opinion," says Bobby Hanna, a safety manager in Hickman who started out as an hourly employee. "It's never a mark against you for trying to do something different if you think it will make things work better," he adds. "It's a mark against you if you don't try."

Speaking for myself, I think the need for freedom is in my genes. I know it's a product of my childhood.

My grandfather was an adventurer who, in his youth, roamed the western United States. He was discharged from the army in 1898 at Yellowstone National Park. My Dad wandered around out west a bit, too. He was a lumberman in Yellowstone and homesteaded a half-section in Montana before coming back to Illinois, where he earned an electrical engineering degree at what was then the Lewis Institute and is now the Illinois Institute of Technology. He then became superintendent of equipment of Western Electric, and had charge of all installations west of the Mississippi. He commuted by train into Chicago each day from Downers Grove, Illinois, the small town where I was raised.

But about every other summer, Dad would load my mother, brother, and me into his car (a 1927 Buick) and drive west to the old homestead in Montana. We'd stay in a little schoolhouse on land my father had donated to the county, and spend a week or so hiking and camping under the Big Sky. Dad willed that homestead to me. Being out in all that open space, it's hard to think *too* highly of yourself.

———■-■-■———

I'M OFTEN ASKED: "How do you explain Nucor's success?" My stock reply: "It is 70% culture and 30% technology." The truth is, I'm not sure if it's 80 to 20 or 60 to 40 percent, but I'm certain our culture accounts for more than half of our success as a business.

Equality, freedom, and mutual respect promote motivation, initiative, and continuous improvement.

Without a doubt, Nucor's culture is its most important source of competitive advantage, and always will be.

Of course, every company has the same opportunity to build a culture that yields competitive advantage. Yet remarkably few seem to act on that opportunity. One reason, I think, is that the culture has to be consistent to be real. Consistency is the name of the game, as far as I'm concerned.

Consistency begins with really believing in the culture you hope to shape. Nucor is founded on principles so basic, they sound corny. We believe in treating people the way you'd want to be treated. That's a fundamental building block of our company. It sounds simplistic, but it works.

Don't think, though, that maintaining such a culture is easy. It demands daily attention to combat our worst human tendencies to divide ourselves into camps of "*We* vs. *They*."

Many executives never take up that fight. They stay in their ivory tower offices. They keep their distance from their people. And that distance breeds arrogance.

Our basic idea is to have the top managers live *in* the operations they manage. That sets the tone. A Nucor general manager sees the good, bad, and ugly of the business every day. He feels the pain and the joy. He sees what people really *do* to make the business go. And that keeps him from getting too big a head, unlike those executives who say, "I'm here to serve the company" as they climb into their limo. I'm not saying that those executives are lying. I guess they really believe that they stand for equality. They're just so isolated, and their egos are so swollen, they've lost sight of what treating others as equals really means.

To managers and executives who sincerely would like to build a culture similar to the one we've built at Nucor, and to gain the competitive advantages we enjoy as a result, I'd offer just this one piece of advice: Be a part of your company. Never set yourself above it.

4

The Engines of Progress

"When I first came to work here, we could produce maybe thirty tons of steel a day, and I'm talkin' a *good* day," recalls Benny Gaincy, who left the tobacco fields in 1969 to take a job at Nucor Steel in Darlington, South Carolina. "Back then, if you'd told me we would find ways to turn out a *hundred* tons of steel in an *hour*, right here in this same mill, I'd have laughed in your face. But that's just what we've done." Benny shakes his head in wonder. "After all I've seen, I wouldn't put anything past us. I'd say the sky's the limit."

Timothy Patterson is a 23-year-old engineer at Nucor-Yamato Steel in Blytheville, Arkansas. He worked summers at the mill while he was earning his degree, so he knows his way around, and when an idea pops into his head he's inclined to share it with somebody. "That's one reason I wanted to be an engineer here instead of someplace else," Tim says. "Some guys still treat me like I was their little brother. But they've always listened, even to a punk kid like me."

Good thing. Last year, Tim calculated that we were spending about $1.5 million annually to lubricate and maintain a series of supporting screws under the Nucor-Yamato rolling line. He noted that shims (tapered pieces of metal) would require no lubrication, and that they might work even better than the screws designed into the equipment by the manufacturer. Turned out to be a pretty smart suggestion. It cut our downtime significantly and is saving us more than a million dollars a year in maintenance costs.

In Crawfordsville, crane operator Calvin Stephens has worked on an arrangement of pneumatic pumps, like shock absorbers, to keep strips of steel centered as they move from a roller to a cutting machine. "It's just a way to speed things up a little," he says. "I figure we could save us a good six or seven seconds on every finished coil of steel. Over a year, we'll be saving a lot of time and putting out more product with the same resources."[1]

I offer those three anecdotes to set the record straight, in some small measure. I've been personally credited with such achievements as demonstrating that the mini-mill concept was commercially viable, with the success of our joint venture with the Japanese firm Yamato Kogyo, and with making the breakthrough thin slab casting technology work at our mill in Crawfordsville.

All incorrect.

It was people like Benny Gainey, who came into Darlington each day to build better molds, and Tim Patterson, who looked past what was already working at Nucor-Yamato to find what might work even better, and Calvin Stephens, who restlessly searches for ways to shave seconds off a work process. *They* did it. Not just the three of them, of course. The credit for most Nucor achievements rightfully belongs to hundreds of people you'd find throughout the company.

At some level, everyone understands that. Yet you don't see *Fortune, BusinessWeek*, or *Industry Week* chasing after Benny, Tim, or Calvin for interviews. They come to the boss. And somehow or other the stories end up giving most of the credit for what a company does to the handful of people who *set* the company's goals, while saying next to nothing about all those people who go out and *fulfill* them.

Granted, business reporters can't interview a couple of thousand employees to find out why a company is growing and making profits. But do they have to turn CEOs into celebrities? If sportswriters covered the Kentucky Derby the way the business press reports on corporate America, we might never have heard of Secretariat, and the guy who owned the stables would be on the cover of *Sports Illustrated*, wearing one of those big wreaths around his neck.

Historians do much the same thing. As children we learned that "Andrew Carnegie built the steel industry" and "Henry Ford built the automotive industry." Carnegie and Ford were, without question, giants. But to suggest that any individual—even a giant—"built" an industry is hogwash. The most any manager can do is shape an environment that allows employees to fulfill the goals of the business.

—■-■-■—

OK, SO MAYBE your face has never graced the cover of *Fortune*. But the inordinate credit our society gives to top business executives can still skew your perspective. Seeing executives so consistently and credibly cast as the major factor in business success, you may assume a mantle of self-importance, simply because you belong to that indispensable fraternity called management. Worse yet, you may give yourself a correspondingly disproportionate share of the credit for getting things done at the level where you work. You can be seduced into forgetting how completely dependent you are on the people whom you manage.

In fact, it seems to me that a lot of managers have *already* forgotten. How else can you explain their attitude toward employees? Across corporate America, at all levels of management, you'll find managers who withhold information and even their attention from the people who work for them, except when they deem to correct or criticize employee actions. Rarely will these managers stoop to solicit an employee's advice on an important issue, entrust employees to independently carry out crucial assignments, or challenge employees to do more than they, the managers themselves, have been able to do.

If you worked for such managers, how important would you feel? Would you think management knew who you really are and what you really could do? Would you believe that you have a chance to make a difference in the business? Most significantly, how long would you go on even *trying* to make a difference?

If you think I'm engaging in a little armchair psychology, you're right. Every manager should be something of a psychologist. We're supposed to know what makes people tick, what they want, and what they need. And much of what people want and need resides in the subconscious.

I've found that, as employees, many people want first and foremost to be appreciated for who they are. They want to be acknowledged as unique individuals—each with immense and unrealized potential. All too often, though, their managers cast them as drones. Small wonder so many employees are emotionally detached from their jobs. They move through the workday like zombies—numb, blank-faced, waiting for quitting time, so they can resume living.

Most managers, meanwhile, worry more than they might admit (or even realize) about where they stand with employees. Employees are people, after all, and people are complex, challenging, unpredictable. Invite them to speak their minds, make decisions, and take on meaningful responsibilities, and who knows where it might lead? My guess is that managers who exhibit the most egotistical, closed, and "authoritative" exteriors often feel, somewhere within, that their hold on authority is tenuous. In a misguided attempt to maintain control, they downgrade their perception of their employees from thinking human beings to something smaller and less threatening. They tell themselves that employees "can't see the big picture" and so "don't really know what's important." And they fulfill their own prophecy by hoarding information.

Worse yet, managers often expand their own egos to fill the void. They become "the brains" of the operation, taking responsibility for all the analysis, problem solving, and decision making. They limit employees to doing what management specifically requires, and nothing more.

That may be a recipe for disaster. Employees—not managers—are the engines of progress. If you keep them stuck in second gear, your business will perform below its true potential, especially over the long term. I believe that this is precisely what is happening, to varying degrees, across many businesses today.

So what's the solution, group therapy for managers and their employees? No, it's simpler than that. All you have to do is go back to the question I posed a moment ago: If you invite your employees to really speak their minds, make critically important decisions, and take on crucial responsibilities, where might it lead? But this time, make a conscious effort to block anxiety from rushing in with visions of chaos. Turn the question over to your *curiosity*, to the "blue sky" thinker within you. Picture your employees pursuing goals—the goals you have set—with a fervor that goes beyond what you would dare ask of them. Envision them doing wonderful things that will make you look very smart. Focus on the *up*side. Wouldn't you like to know just how good things could really be?

I GAINED AN especially revealing glimpse into how good things could be while I was general manager at Coast Metals in Little Ferry, New Jersey, in the early 1960s. The shop where we ground welding rods was a gloomy place. So I collared an electrician one afternoon and told him: "Let's light this place up. Give me sixty lumens in this room."

Two weeks later, the electrician popped into my office. "The new lights are in. Want to see them come on?" He looked so excited, I could hardly refuse.

It was the middle of a shift, so the place was full and plenty busy. Nobody noticed us at the door. "Ready?" asked the electrician, rubbing his hands together in anticipation. "Yeah, sure. Do it," I said. With a showman's touch, the electrician reached over and threw four newly installed switches, one switch at a time.

As the lights came up, everything in the shop stopped. A few workers blinked and shook their heads, like prisoners unexpectedly released from some medieval dungeon. Most just smiled.

The whole character of the room changed. I realized that the workplace shapes people's state of mind. But I'd never witnessed such a definitive transition. The electrician stood with his hands on his hips, feeling heroic. I didn't blame him.

Then, something extraordinary happened. A worker looked around, looked at the mess, picked up a broom, and started to sweep the shop. Quite by accident, we'd induced someone to *voluntarily* sweep the floor. That's the kind of job most workers resent. If I'd asked him to do it, he'd probably have said he was too busy or, at best, done it grudgingly. But when we adjusted the work environment, this fellow's first instinct was to do precisely what he'd resist doing if it was management's idea. Could it really be that easy?

In a sense, it is. As anyone who has taken a management course knows, researchers proved years ago that increased lighting can lead to increased productivity. More broadly, their studies showed that the work *environment* can have a profound effect on work *performance*.

I've found that people's desire to improve, achieve, and contribute are virtually universal. Very few employees are apathetic by nature. However, they can be *conditioned* into apathy by their environments. (For proof of that, observe people at work in most big corporations. You'll find plenty.)

I should stress that by "environment" I mean the cultural as well as the physical world in which people work. The ideas, attitudes, and assumptions that surround them are *as* critical—and are often *more* critical.

What's really astounding, though, is how few managers actually stop and think about the role of the environment—physical and cultural. After all, shaping the work environment is an acknowledged part of the manager's responsibility. And it stands to reason that environments that suppress initiative, innovation, motivation, and teamwork could be redesigned to promote those qualities.

Yet many managers are so wrapped up in themselves, they ignore the impact of environment altogether. I think managers should tinker with the work environment, day in and day out, to learn what people can do and will do, given the right conditions. All through my management career, I've tried to guess what changes might bring out more of the imaginative, energetic, complex people with whom I work. It is a form of ongoing experimentation. And it has proved fascinating as well as rewarding.

At Coast Metals, for example, we were getting too many rejects in some castings we manufactured for use in building aircraft. Normally, management would bring defects to workers' attention, then give them specific instructions on how to improve the quality of their work.

But in this instance, the foreman and I hauled a big red bench to the middle of the foundry floor and piled on all the rejects for the day. We left it there and went about our own business. Some of the workers came over to see what this was about. They checked out the rejects and talked among themselves about why the castings weren't meeting specs, shortly concluding that most of the rejects were the result of molding mistakes—i.e., preventable errors. Well, that started them trading ideas on how to bring the reject rate down, which they did, without so much as a word from the foreman or me. At the end of six weeks, very few castings were finding their way to the red bench.

All we, the management, did was bring attention to the serious errors that were being made, in a way that brought it home. But we pulled up short of telling them what to do about it. We were conceding that maybe, just maybe, the employees might develop a better solution to the problem than could management. How often do managers do that?

At Nucor, employees are a conscious party to such experiments. Most everyone who sticks with Nucor is intrigued by human potential—their own and that of the people working around them. They'd much rather be stimulated and challenged by their environment than be confined to a job description.

"When we decided to build a second rolling mill here, they made me coordinator for the design and construction of the meltshop," says Greg Mathis, a meltshop supervisor at Nucor-Yamato. "I really didn't know what I was getting into. They put it all on my shoulders—the planning, the engineering, the contracting, the budgets . . . I mean, we're talking about an investment of millions of dollars, and I was accountable for *all* of it. I'd never taken on anything so big before. It worked out fine, though, because we were working with good contractors who knew what to do, and because my team and I knew what *not* to do, from our experience running the meltshop on the first line. We were able to head off all the stuff that the engineers think is great but turns out to be just a pain in the butt to us."

Nucor employees realize that by experimenting with the work environment and throwing them big challenges, my fellow managers and I are really working for them. We're trying to open new possibilities for employees to innovate and achieve. And most of the time, that is what happens. Employees become the engines of progress.

"I almost never go out there and say, 'Boy, I've got a great idea,' " says Kevin Young, manager of our cold mill in Crawfordsville. "Virtually every improvement we've made has come from the operators and the operating supervisors. We just make sure they get implemented."[2]

Here's a twist for you: By delegating most major areas of responsibility, focusing our attention on shaping the work environment so employees can find most of the answers without our help, and conceding that we, the managers, don't always know just what the heck we're doing, we seem to have earned more credibility and authority than we could ever gain by acting like bosses.

—∎∎∎—

Can you go overnight from acting like a boss to managing as we do at Nucor? Probably not. You have to be realistic about the obstacles you may encounter along the way.

Most of today's corporations were conceived as command-and-control organizations. The founders of integrated steel mills, for example, clearly assumed that the "genius" of the organization resided almost completely in management. By design, employees were restricted to roles rigidly defined by a few people at the top. In most corporations, in fact, a command-and-control mind set has been in place for so long, it may not be easy to entice employees into sharing more of their genius.

In contrast, we built Nucor under the assumption that most of the "genius" in our organization would be found among the people doing the work. From the outset, we shaped our business to let employees show management the way to goals that once seemed unreachable.[3] I admit, that makes it easier and probably more consistently rewarding for us to manage in the ways I've described.

I see evidence that a lot of businesses are trying to move in a direction that would make it easier for their managers to manage as we do at Nucor. Business leaders increasingly recognize that their people are a severely underutilized resource. I hear executives say words to that effect, often enough. More reliably, U.S. businesses spend more than $55 billion each year on human resource training and development.[4] That tells me that business in general now senses a pretty significant opportunity to tap into more of employees' potential.

What most businesses haven't figured out, it appears, is just *how* to pursue that opportunity. They've made enormous investments in management fads, quality circles, reengineering, restructuring, writing vision statements, and the like, hoping to increase efficiency, productivity, and flexibility. The results have been questionable. There's been plenty of disappointment and disillusion. Lots of programs have been thrown out.

Things won't get much better, I'm afraid, until those businesses drill all the way down to their seminal ideas about management: "Managers hold the key to business success." "Managers are the brains of the operation." "Managers must command, control, and micromanage the business." If businesses hope to find out what employees can really do, that is the level where the change must begin.

—■■■—

Maybe the next generation of *senior* managers will drive more meaningful change than did the last. Will you be a part of that next generation? Perhaps. But only if you understand what it takes to get there.

Performing well in your current position only qualifies you for consideration. To demonstrate you're destined for a top job, you must constructively stir things up. Envision what the company could be if the conditions were changed. Start to talk about how things might be done *differently*. Maybe you can't change how you're required to manage overnight. But you can certainly start to *advocate* change.

What changes should you advocate? I can't see the future. But it seems very probable that conditions will increasingly favor businesses that draw extraordinarily high levels of performance from their people.

You can help others see that, by clinging to the vestiges of "command-and-control" management, a business blocks the vast majority of its people from making those and other critical contributions. You can become a proponent of spreading more information to employees, giving them more responsibility for generating ideas, and increasing their decision-making powers. You can help your business understand what it takes to make employees engines of progress. A few examples:

Choosing the Right People. Not every employee wants his or her work to be challenging, and not every manager will entrust major decision-making authority to employees. So, if you want employees to assume more responsibility for business success, you must make the capacity for innovation, flexibility, creativity, power-sharing, and so forth a clear priority in hiring and in weighing candidates for promotion. Often, that means changing how you screen candidates.

We've worked, for example, with a consultant out of Chicago, Dr. John Seres, to develop tests for our candidates to become Nucor supervisors. The questions are heterogeneous and many seem irrelevant—e.g., "Do you like to go to baseball games?" "How many hours a night do you like to sleep?"—but a candidate's responses will tell us with fair reliability whether he or she is likely to succeed as a Nucor supervisor.

Reallocating Managers' Time. Managers typically spend far more time planning, instructing, and inspecting than they do listening, experimenting, and analyzing. Your company's managers will have to reverse that ratio to make their employees engines of progress.

Letting Employees Guide Their Own Development. As employees take on more and more responsibility, management must give them more development opportunities and more development latitude.

At Nucor, virtually all our employees are cross-trained to do multiple jobs. And when they see an opportunity to improve their abilities—whether through training, tackling a new kind of project, or spending time in another facility—

they fully expect their managers to help them make it happen.

Providing Information to Employees. When you make employees primarily responsible for the success of a business, they demand more access to information. That's only natural. They need it. At Nucor, our official information policy is to "share everything."

You can become a proponent of spreading more information to employees and of helping them use that information to become engines of progress.

Letting Employees Invest in Technology. Are your senior managers ready to let someone else make most decisions as to what technology is worthy of investment? Well, it's time for them to get ready. This has been a crucial element of Nucor's success, at any rate.

Most people still think of steel making as an old-line "rust belt" industry. But walk through our mills and you'll find complex melting and rolling systems run by computers that make hundreds of minute adjustments each second; lasers taking measurements down to thousandths of an inch; and custom products conforming to incredibly tight, customer-defined specs. People in the mills identified and selected most of that technology.

That's the way it has to be. When you put the burden of staying competitive on your employees, you owe it to them to provide the best tools available. Besides, technology is advancing too quickly on too many fronts. No small group of executives can possibly keep fully informed. You have to let people decide for themselves which tools are best, then hold them accountable for their decisions.

Weighing Mergers and Acquisitions from Employees' Perspective. A lot of corporations jump into new businesses, make acquisitions, and even decide to merge based on very questionable criteria like "favorable ratios," "minimal redundancy," and (my personal favorite) "strategic synergism." Perhaps that's why more than half of such moves eventually fail—"strategic synergism" often turns out to be what I'd call "b.s. synergism." Ratios or no ratios, the people of the company have no idea how to make the new business or the newly merged organization work. Furthermore, acquisitions can rob your business of needed resources.

The more you rely on employees to drive business success, the more circumspect you must be about every major move. How might an acquisition, for example, affect your work environment? Could it detract from your people's motivation, initiative, and productivity? Will you have to strap your employees for resources to fund senior management's shopping spree?

We have made very few acquisitions. We tend to build businesses from the ground up. But we make plenty of big decisions, and we try to look at every big decision from our employees' perspective, as well as from the perspective of our shareholders and customers. We want everything we do to make sense to our people, because we know that we'll rely on them to make each move work.

Our decision to go into the bolt manufacturing business is a case in point. By 1985, big steel companies like Bethlehem Steel, Armco Steel, and Republic Steel were all quitting on the bolt and fastener business. It sure wasn't for lack of a market. The automotive industry alone used more than 25 billion bolts a year. The problem was costs. The companies that stopped manufacturing bolts were using fifty-year-old manufacturing technology and union labor. They couldn't come close to imported products on price.

We thought we could. It was a steel business, and we knew something about producing steel products at competitive costs, even while paying our people top dollar. Management saw that, and our employees would see it, too. So we launched the Nucor Fastener division in St. Joe, Indiana, and equipped it with the latest technology. While the old-line manufacturers had one or two men making fifty bolts per minute, we had one man operating four machines making 400 bolts per minute. Before long, St. Joe was turning a healthy profit. It still is.

Our employees succeeded where others had failed. That surprised a lot of people, I suppose, but not us, because we'd sized the opportunity up from our employees' perspective.

—■■■—

THE GREAT AND TERRIBLE irony of modern business is that so many managers feel overburdened with responsibility, while so many employees feel unchallenged and unfulfilled in their jobs.

The way to a happier and more prosperous state is clear: Concede once and for all that employees, not managers, are the true engines of progress, and dedicate your management career to creating an environment in which employees can stretch for higher and higher levels of performance.

Shaping the work environment has always been an acknowledged part of the manager's responsibility. But to my way of thinking, it's the manager's *primary* job. Instead of telling people what to do and then hounding them to do it, our managers focus on shaping an environment that frees employees to determine what they can do and should do, to the benefit of themselves and the business. We've found that *their* answers drive the progress of our business faster than our own.

Is there a better way for managers to invest their time and energy? I doubt it. The manager who devotes him or herself to this endeavor is on the side of the angels. Employees will sincerely appreciate your efforts to help them explore and develop their capabilities. Customers and investors will appreciate the superior performance of your employees and, as a direct result, of your business. Last but not least, you and your fellow managers will appreciate all the fine things people will say and write about you. True, it'll be more than you deserve. But is that your fault?

5

A Simple Stake in the Business

EARLY IN 1985, Nucor Steel in Darlington, South Carolina, ran a little classified ad in the local newspaper. It read: "Nucor Steel in Darlington will take some applications for new employees on Saturday morning at 8:30." That's all. As it turned out, we might as well have run an ad saying, "Nucor Steel in Darlington will give away some big-screen color TVs."

On the morning of the interviewing, our general manager in Darlington found the mill's access road jammed with cars and pickup trucks. Hundreds of able-bodied men had turned out to apply for our eight openings. The line of applicants stretched halfway around the plant. These were not desperate times. Most of these men already had jobs someplace else, or could have them if they wanted. Yet they had climbed out of bed on a Saturday morning to stand outside a steel mill in the stiff March wind. It was a tough way to spend a weekend.

A few applicants huddled here and there to trade stories, but most were alone with their thoughts. A wiry little fellow stood with his shoulders square and his arms resting straight by his sides. His posture indicated patience, but he gazed wistfully toward the front of the line. He'd probably spent time in the military. He knew how to wait. A bit farther back, a young guy, not yet twenty, leaned into the chain-link fence, hands pushed deep into the pockets of his jeans. For him, this was likely a crash course in marking time. Those from the middle of the line on back wouldn't get inside the mill for hours. Yet these were men on a mission. They weren't about to give up and go home.

Our general manager, realizing that he and his personnel people couldn't get in the plant, went back out to the main road and called the Highway Patrol. "Could you send someone out to the mill?" he asked. "We have one heck of a big crowd here."

"We'll send someone as soon as we can," replied the officer who answered the call. "But we're short-handed this morning. Three of our people are there applying for jobs with you!"

A Simple Stake in the Business

—■■■—

WORKING IN A steel mill isn't what most of us would call a cushy job. So why did all those people line up for positions at Nucor? We were offering the opportunity to earn more than most people could earn anywhere else in the area.

I'll let you in on a little secret: Most people will work hard for money! In fact, we find that motivating people boils down to: *a*) the opportunity to earn an above-average income; *b*) job security; and *c*) opportunities for advancement. You can pretty much throw away "good training," "clean bathrooms," and the rest of the list of what motivates employees. Without good pay, job security, and opportunities for advancement, those other things won't mean very much.

If that's not a secret, it might as well be. Most businesses vastly underutilize money as a *day-to-day* motivator. They set a strict budget for what they're willing to pay people in wages and salaries, then they squeeze as much work as they can out of their people for that fixed number of dollars.

I don't know why any employer would expect much from this approach. Look at it from the employees' perspective—they come to work each day knowing exactly how much they will earn. And when you get right down to it, all they must do to get that amount is not get fired. Work hard today or hardly work at all, and the pay is the same. So tell me, where's the *day-to-day* motivation to work harder and smarter?

In fact, Nucor CFO Sam Siegel contends that managers should view underpaid employees as a *cost*— and a very high one at that—because people who are dissatisfied with their pay are always on the lookout for a chance to avoid work. When the boss is out of sight, they sneak in a nap. A sneeze becomes a reason to stay home.

At Nucor, we never know exactly how much we'll have to pay our people for their day's work. The sky's the limit. For their part, our employees start each day with no guarantee that they'll earn a competitive wage, because base pay for Nucor production jobs is usually set below the industry average.

The key is, base pay is just a fraction of what our people have the opportunity to earn. Nucor production employees can also earn weekly bonuses, above and beyond base pay. In recent years, weekly bonuses have run from 100 percent to over 200 percent of base pay in our steel mills. That means a typical production employee might earn eight or nine dollars per hour in base pay *plus* more than sixteen dollars an hour in production bonuses. Nucor production workers earned an average of more than $60,000 in 1996. They're the best-paid employees in the industry.

What must employees do to earn their weekly bonus? Two things: *a*) work in teams; *b*) produce!

A Simple Stake in the Business

A production baseline is established for groups of twenty to forty people who together perform some complete task. Any production above and beyond that baseline earns each member of the work group bonus pay.

Take a melting and casting crew in one of our steel mills, for example. Shifts of 20–25 workers melt down scrap metal and then cast it into "billets" (semi-finished products which we then roll into steel bars or angles). Production of billets is a clear process with a measurable output. The production baseline, for example, may be set at fifty tons of good billets per hour, and the group may have the opportunity to earn a bonus of 4 percent of base pay for every ton of good billets it produces above and beyond the baseline. So, if the group averages one hundred tons per hour over the course of a workweek, each member receives a bonus of 200 percent of base pay (50 tons over baseline × 4 percent = 200 percent). The 200 percent bonus is paid along with regular base paychecks the following Thursday.

We take care to set a realistic production figure as a baseline for these teams—a tonnage they have to work reasonably hard to achieve but which is definitely within their reach. We *want* the teams to get a taste of the bonus because, once they do, they always stretch for more.

I recall that we started a crew on a straightener machine—which straightens steel angles to meet our customers' requirements—at a production bonus baseline of eight tons per hour. The rated capacity of the machine was ten tons per hour. Well, that crew kept tinkering and experimenting. They installed a larger motor, fed the angles into the machine in various ways, and so on. Within a year, their production was up to twenty tons an hour, twice that machine's rated capacity. Perhaps the engineers who calculate a machine's capacity should come up with a new formula, one that estimates the capacity of machines run by people who earn according to what they produce.

"Most businesses focus on what a person *makes*," notes Ham Lott, general manager of Vulcraft in Florence. "We think what matters is how much labor cost goes into the product. If we pay our people twice what a competitor pays, but that opportunity to earn more motivates them to produce three times as many joists per hour, our joists cost less."

Our employment cost in 1996 (including fringe benefits) was less than $40 per ton of steel produced, roughly half the total employment cost per ton produced by the big steel companies. Our people earn more because they're more efficient and more productive. We didn't make them that way. We just structured compensation to give them a clear incentive and turned them loose. We've trusted in their ingenuity to keep us competitive. And they haven't let us down.

A Simple Stake in the Business

The real beauty of Nucor's compensation system, in my opinion, is that *there is nothing to discuss.* Daily output and corresponding bonus earnings are posted, so employees know exactly what their bonus will be before they tear open their pay envelopes. No judgment. No negotiation. No surprises.

A version of Nucor's production bonus system was in place at Vulcraft when I became manager of the Florence, South Carolina, plant in 1962. It seemed to work well there, so we refined it and brought it into the other divisions, including our new steel mills. As I remember it, the first time a production bonus was over 100 percent, I thought we'd created a monster. In a lot of companies, I imagine the managers would have said, "Whoops, we didn't set that up right. We'd better change it." Then, they'd probably bring in some consultant to justify backing out of the deal. Not us. We've modified it some over the years. But we've stuck with that basic concept ever since.

The gist of that concept is that the company supplies the equipment, training, benefits program, and other fundamental support, and leaves the rest up to the group. So, in a sense, each group is in business for itself. Work groups set their own goals for exceeding the baseline and work out their own ways of pursuing them, guided only by this certainty: The more they produce, the more they earn. They have a simple stake in the business.

Like most successful entrepreneurs, our employees are enthusiastic, energetic, and dead earnest about their work. "If your shift starts at two o'clock, you should be here by one or one-fifteen. The latest anybody on our team shows up is one-thirty," says Tony Myers, a production worker from our Vulcraft plant in Florence. "We get all our equipment ready. We talk about what we have to do to make things go right. It's like a football team before a game. You don't show up for the kickoff. You get there early and you get yourself ready. When that horn blows, we have to be primed. We've got eight hours to make us some money. The more we get done, the more we make."

Steel joists are a key component of the metal skeleton that supports most industrial, commercial, and institutional buildings. We fabricate joists to the specs provided by construction engineers for a specific project. Joist manufacture is something of a specialty, so the automation options are limited. You need people, working in teams, to do it right.

Ham Lott calls the rigging table and welding pit—successive stations on the Vulcraft line where Tony Myers works—"the best show of labor in the United States." A partially assembled open web joist comes rattling down the line. Six riggers quickly heft the 30'–50' frame onto the rigging table and start clamping the metal angles into place, custom-forming the complex structure called for in a schematic, which each team member has studied. In less than a minute, the joist is ready to move down the line to the welding pit, where the crew of eight converges on it like the tentacles of a highly synchronized machine. Safety masks flip down and torches flare brilliant white as the workers apply a series of precise welds. Speed is everything. Yet speed without accuracy is nothing. A quality inspection waits at the next station. Miss a weld, and the joist may be rejected, and yield no bonus to the group.

What about the supervisor? "You wouldn't know who the supervisor is by watching us work," Tony says. "He's part of the team. He shares in the same bonus. He's not worried about being the big man in charge. He's worried about making things so we can all earn more money. We're all looking at this the same."

The pressure to perform is intense, but virtually all of it comes from peers—the other members of the group—rather than from anyone in management.

"If you're the last man welding, or if you're screwing up your welds, everybody knows. And you better believe they get on you, too," Tony says. "The company gives a new guy on the crew ninety days to prove himself. But we know in about a month if he's going to make it. At first, we just tell him things. Explain what he needs to know. We work hard at training him because, if we do, he's going to make us some money. If a guy won't work, though, the team will run him off. It's not about liking him or not liking him. It's about making a living. That man's gotta make it or break it.

"I heard once that if you have a team of mules and horses, the horses will make the mules work," Tony says. "I'm a horse. I'm not the fastest or the best. But I can float around and keep up with any job on the line. And I can talk while I work," he adds with a smile. "You gotta be able to do that if you want to be a horse. Other guys talk some, too. But most stay quiet. They're concentrating. I yell at them. Sometimes they yell back. Nobody gets mad, though. We're all just trying to make some money. At the end of the shift, we'll just sit down and laugh about it."

Maintenance personnel participate in the production bonus right along with the rest of the crew. You won't find maintenance and production people working more closely together in any manufacturing facility anywhere in the world. "Our goal is to help production people make as much money as they can each week, because that's how we make as much as we can," says Jake Schmidt, maintenance manager at Nucor Steel in Darlington. "It works the other way, too," Jake adds. "Everyone in this mill—not just the maintenance guys—has a clear incentive to keep the machinery humming along smoothly."

Nucor's engineers, secretaries, clerks, receptionists, and other nonproduction employees have their own bonus plan, keyed to their division's return on assets employed. This encourages them to be efficient in their own work, to build and maintain strong customer relationships for the division, and to do whatever they can to help the people who produce our products. Bonuses for nonproduction employees run up to 25 percent of base pay in some divisions, but the bonus in some divisions may be zero if they don't generate an adequate return.

Nucor department managers—the six to eight managers in charge of the main functions or operations within each division—also earn annual incentive bonuses based primarily on the contribution to earnings (technically, return on assets employed) made by their division, with a small additional bonus keyed to the performance of the corporation overall. Department managers can earn bonuses of up to 82 percent of base pay. But in some years, the department managers in some Nucor divisions have received no bonus at all.

Nucor officers receive a base salary that is typically just 75 percent of that earned by executives in comparable positions across manufacturing. The remainder of their compensation is variable and entirely at risk, just like the production bonus.

At the officer level, Nucor ties bonus compensation to return on shareholder's equity—a vital performance measure watched closely by most stockholders. The more earnings our company returns to investors, the more money our officers earn.

The baseline for our officers' bonus is set at the exceptional end of the scale for return on shareholder's equity. The average Fortune 500 company earns about an 11 to 12 percent return on shareholder's equity. Our officers' bonus doesn't kick in until the company achieves a return of 8 percent on shareholder's equity, and is capped at 24 percent of shareholder's equity, at which point officers receive a bonus of about 200 percent of their base pay in cash plus a bonus of 100 percent of base pay in stock. We've reached that maximum about three or four years out of the past twenty, and three or four years our officers have earned no bonus at all.

———■-■-■———

AT MOST MAJOR corporations today, executive compensation is outrageous. I'm not just referring to the amounts of money snatched up by a few individuals when their companies make money. Even more disturbing is how executives constantly abuse their power to shield themselves from harsh reality. They give themselves big bonuses and raises (rubber stamped, of course, by their boards) even when the companies they lead lose money. They claim that their compensation is "tied to the goals of the company." But much of the time, that's just nonsense. For it to be true, the goal of the company would have to be, "Pay our executives lots of money, come hell or high water."

As a shareholder, I think that money should go back into the business. The company needs it more. Besides, when executives face the possibility of a downside, it keeps them focused on achieving the upside.

———■·■·■———

I'VE SPENT THE better part of this chapter describing Nucor's approach to compensation, because I think it is one of the most critical elements of our company's success. Now let's talk about your company.

Maybe your company's employees do work that is so different from making steel or assembling steel joists, there is no way you could implement a Nucor-type production bonus. And maybe people in your company are less motivated by opportunities to earn more money. They have other priorities. Does that mean your company can't find ways to make compensation more motivating for its employees? Isn't the question at least worth exploring?

Now you may be thinking, "That's easy for you to say, Mr. Chairman. But I'm just a middle manager. Nobody asks *me* what I think of our company's compensation system." Well, who says you have to wait to be asked? I never knew a good manager who didn't take a bull by the horns once in a while, including bulls that are too big for any middle manager to handle alone.

In most companies, there are a few executives who, as a matter of principle, habitually question the status quo. Start there. You don't have to storm in on them like some kind of crusader. There's no need to attack your company's compensation system. Just go in as a manager who poses thoughtful questions.

You might start, for example, with: "We've been searching up and down for ways to make this business perform better. That got me to wondering, when was the last time we took a hard look at how we structure employee compensation? Not the details of compensation . . . the *basics?*"

No matter how the executive feels about the current compensation approach, he or she would likely admit: "That's a pretty good question."

You can then step in with more good questions. Good managers are supposed to ponder possibilities beyond their areas of immediate authority. They are supposed to be students of the business. A smart way to frame your questions about compensation, then, is with the phrase "I wonder." A few examples:

"I wonder if we couldn't find ways to get a little more motivation and productivity in return for our compensation dollars?"

"I wonder how many people here feel truly challenged and inspired, day in and day out, by the earning opportunities we currently offer them?"

"I wonder how close a connection employees see between how hard they work each day and what we pay them for their work?"

"I wonder if we couldn't find tangible productivity measures for groups of people where no such measures are apparent for individuals?"

"I wonder if our approach to compensation might be falling a step or two behind the changes we're trying to make . . . Is it doing all it could to advance our initiatives on teamwork, innovation, and cycle time reduction?"

Pose such questions to the right executive, and the reply should be fairly predictable: "I wonder about those things, too." If the executive also says, "We should start finding the answers to those questions," you're no longer "just" a middle manager. You're a middle manager on a mission.

You can rest assured, by the way, that you won't be drawing attention to problems for which there are no solutions. Most compensation systems have ample room for improvement at fundamental, non-technical levels, because most companies give so little thought to the basics of their compensation practices. They take them as a given.

At minimum, most companies' compensation systems could and certainly should be made more objective. I've found that objectivity is closely correlated with fairness in compensation, and who doesn't think compensation should be fair?

I read a story in the paper not long ago. An employee was suing a company over a bonus! It seems the manager had a lower opinion of the employee's performance than did the employee. I thought, "That's what you get for sitting like King Solomon as the great judge of another person." So many businesses use subjective criteria (e.g., "Works well with others," "Takes initiative") to gauge people's performance, I'm surprised employees don't sue more often. How can such a system be fair?

Many businesses go to great lengths to make their subjective systems *appear* to be objective. But rating people on a 1 to 10 scale is not, in and of itself, objective. Such ratings reflect the *judgment* of the person who circles the little numbers on the form. Nothing more.

If I were a manager in one of those companies that makes you rate people using such ridiculously subjective criteria, I'd give everybody a 10. The heck with it. It would serve the company right for putting me in such an absurd position. Besides, I might be saving them from a big lawsuit.

As I've stressed, compensation has also been the key to fostering teamwork in Nucor. All kinds of businesses are trying to encourage teamwork these days, for all kinds of reasons, and with very mixed results. The root of their frustration, I suspect, may be that their compensation systems still reward individual contributions more than they reward teamwork. Some also tie variable compensation to silly goals that have little to do with the real work people must perform for the business to be productive and profitable.

Instead of sending their people off to seminars to close their eyes and fall into one another's arms, maybe these companies should restructure compensation to ensure that people who work together, earn together.

—■-■-■—

LIKE MOST COMPANIES, Nucor offers forms of compensation beyond base pay and bonuses. But we see profit sharing and benefits as secondary, not primary, motivators.

For one thing, most businesses only pay out profit sharing once a year. So, most of the time, it's not on people's minds the way a weekly bonus payment is. We also find that people perceive what they do, day to day, as having a very small effect on the overall profitability of the business. In other words, for the average employee, profit sharing is neither timely nor immediate.

That doesn't mean profit sharing isn't important. We use it as a way to help our employees prepare for their futures and to share in the success of the business. Working men and women can be very well set up when the time comes for them to leave Nucor. Some of our long-term employees have hundreds of thousands of dollars in their retirement accounts.

At the same time, we do what we can to make sure the 10 percent of profits we share each year with employees won't be taken for granted in the short term. I think that happens in companies that simply direct-deposit profit sharing into employees' trust accounts and notify them with some bland computer printout. So we pay out a small amount of each employee's profit share in cash, to remind them that profit sharing is real money. We've even printed out those profit-sharing checks on green paper to reinforce that point.

By the way, Nucor officers are excluded from profit sharing. They have the means to prepare financially for their own retirement and other future events. We focus that program on serving the people who truly depend on it.

Four times, that I can recall, we have paid our employees an extraordinary bonus. We do it only when the company is generating record earnings. And we pay the same amount to every employee. (Officers are excluded.) In distributing the extraordinary bonus, we make it clear that this is an exception, not a precedent.

Once, just after we'd paid an extraordinary bonus of $500 to Nucor employees, Sam Siegel, our CFO, sighed and said to me: "Well, Ken, you just spent $3 million in about fifteen minutes. Do you feel good?" I sure did.

Another important Nucor benefit began in tragedy. Several Nucor workers were killed in an accident on the job in 1974. It was a terrible, terrible time. At the next general managers' meeting, we were still badly shaken over losing some of our own. The worst part was how senseless it seemed. Why did this happen? What have we learned from it? Isn't there anything we can do?

Someone suggested that the company set up a college scholarship program for children of those who had died. Dave Aycock, a former president of Nucor, then said, "No, not just for them. If we do it for one we should do it for all." In 1975, that became our policy. We established a scholarship of $1,000 per year for every child of every Nucor employee (again, excluding officers) to attend four years of college or vocational school. Today, our Scholarship Fund will pay $2,200 a year toward each child's education.

About 700 young people from Nucor families received scholarships this year. The program cost the company nearly $1.4 million in 1996. It's a tremendous benefit, especially for big families.

Of course, it's not entirely altruistic. The company definitely gains, because the program becomes a subject of conversation around the kitchen table. If you want to do something that employees will really appreciate, do something for their families.

Just after we announced the scholarship program in 1975, an employee approached Marv Pullman, our general manager in Darlington, South Carolina, at the time. "You mean to tell me Nucor will give me a thousand dollars a year for four years for *each* of my kids?" the employee asked. Marv assured him it was true. "I have eleven children," the man said. "That's forty-four thousand dollars! There's no way you're going to drive me away."

IT SEEMS TO me that most managers don't think nearly enough about what the business should get in return for its compensation dollar. Either that or they just expect too darn little.

At minimum, pay systems should drive specific behaviors that make your business competitive. So much of what other businesses admire in Nucor—our teamwork, extraordinary productivity, low costs, applied innovation, high morale, low turnover—is rooted in how we pay our people. More than that, our pay and benefit programs tie each employee's fate to the fate of our business. What's good for the company is good—in hard dollar terms—for the employee.

At Nucor, we expect compensation to do more than keep people from quitting. We expect it to give everyone a simple stake in the business.

6

THE VIRTUES OF SMALLNESS

Iɴ 1947, I ʟᴀɴᴅᴇᴅ my first job out of college working as a research physicist with International Harvester (now called Navistar). Like IBM, General Motors, or US Steel at that time, International Harvester was an institution as much as a business, big beyond comprehension, yet benevolent, a righteous titan of progress, a corporate manifestation of the boundless potential and raw might that was post-war America. My ticket had been punched.

It was an interesting job, too. I worked in the physics lab. My duties included operating spectrographic, radiographic, and x-ray defraction equipment, as well as one of the early electron microscopes, an instrument so powerful it could magnify a dime up to the equivalent of an object two-and-a-half miles in diameter.

The Chicago Art Institute once asked our lab to validate the authenticity of some Chinese bronzes they had on display. I went down there and filed some samples from the edges and corners of about twenty-five pieces. Testing with our spectrograph revealed several of them to be fakes. They'd been made out of different base ores than the authentic bronze antiques. One of the fellows at the Art Institute told me that enterprising Chinese sometimes created fake antiques by urinating over buried bronze figures for a number of years. The Art Institute had been taken in by this very scam yet, as far as I know, the pieces we'd shown to be nothing but fakes remained on display.

Another time, we used the electron microscope to show that barb-shaped particles carried by zinc smoke were causing chronic throat irritations among welders. They were subsequently required to wear filtering masks.

My boss at the lab was the chief research physicist, Al Ellis, a blunt, demanding, serious scientist who suffered fools badly.

One day, the chairman of International Harvester was on a tour of the research center, accompanied by his entourage. The electron microscope proved a point of special interest. Al Ellis described the instrument and some of the research we were performing with it.

"With this wonderful instrument," the chairman suggested grandly but naively, "you should be able to find the cold virus." Ellis turned beet red. "Sir, if you gave us $80,000 to set up a research study, we might make a serious start. . . . Did you think we could just put a piece of snot under there and we'd see something waving a little flag that says, 'I am the cold virus'?"

Not very diplomatic of Al, I'll admit, but he was pure scientist, and from the scientist's point of view, the chairman's comment was presumptuous, at best, and probably somewhat insulting. That didn't matter, of course. They got Ellis. They did it gradually, quietly, and methodically (that is, they did it *institutionally*), but they got him. He was passed over for choice assignments. Budgets were tightened. One by one, the doors of opportunity slammed shut. They made him invisible. Two years later, he left the company.

I learned a lot of science from Al Ellis, but the most valuable lessons he taught me were about business, which is surprising, since Ellis wasn't much of a businessman. Al's experience taught me that you can't cross the boss in a big corporation. Being dutiful and good, even excellent, at your job is not enough. The behemoth that provides for you demands more than your honest effort in return. It extracts a measure of your individuality, as well. That was the deal.

Al Ellis also gave me a piece of advice that changed my life. He said: "You can spend your whole career in this environment and you won't end up very satisfied. If you really want to do things in business, you'd be better off going into a small company that will let you get some real business experience."

It was the best advice I've ever received from anyone other than my father. I left International Harvester the next year to take a job with Illium Corporation, a small foundry. I've never regretted that step out of the mega-corporation's embrace. It carried me into a different world.

—■-■-■—

"BIGGER IS BETTER." That is an underlying assumption in business. Companies constantly boast that "We are the world's largest," as if being big alone makes them superior. College graduates vie for positions in mega-corporations, blindly assuming that a big business will offer them better career opportunities and more security. Corporations gain substantial and tangible prestige from being named to the Fortune 500, although the sole criterion for making the list is size. Executives plow hard-earned assets into building monstrous corporate headquarters. . . . You get the idea. "Bigger." "Better." In business, the words might as well be synonyms.

In some ways, of course, they are. Customers often choose big suppliers over small ones, simply because they feel more confident working with "the market leaders." IBM once conquered the world by exploiting that very tendency. Even at Nucor, where some of us have spent the better part of our careers battling and bashing "BIG STEEL," we often brag that we are now "the third-largest steel maker in America."

Businesspeople's overwhelming bias toward bigness is understandable. Size offers some obvious advantages. But it is not a guarantee of business success. Southwest Airlines proved that. Seeing that the big air carriers were locked into their own rules and traditions, Southwest jumped into the fray with its no-frills, low-cost, on-time service. The fact that it was much smaller than its established competitors didn't stop Southwest from carving out an unusually profitable niche in the airline industry. In fact, smallness lent Southwest the freedom to innovate and ensured the low cost structure required to do the job. Southwest (like Nucor) consistently makes money, although it competes in an industry that's often awash in red ink.

When Nucor entered the steel-making business in 1967, we were very small in comparison to the big steel companies, and it was widely assumed that we could never take the big boys on head-to-head. Nucor battling Bethlehem Steel would be like a flea going after a rhinoceros. At best, we might find room to operate on the fringes of the industry.

That is, in fact, how we began. We made relatively simple products like steel bars that were not very important to the big steel producers. But we eventually produced a wider range of products, brazenly invading turf that the behemoths were determined to keep for themselves. No matter. Although the big steel companies have fought us tooth and nail, we've been able to wrest away and hold significant shares of their markets. How? Cost efficiency, flexibility, and innovation. We're further proof that bigger is not necessarily better in business competition.

No one can deny, then, that smallness has its virtues. Yet, in practice, managers often fixate on the advantages of size. Don't fall into that trap! Take a balanced view. Look for ways to make the strengths of size *and* the virtues of smallness work for you.

If you are a young manager still choosing your career path, for example, consider the advantages which only a small business can offer. I can tell you from experience, working in a small company lets you get your hands on *everything*. You can actually see how the whole business fits together, end to end. You'll learn about operations, accounting, research, marketing, sales . . . and that breadth of perspective will prepare you for just about anything you're likely to encounter down the road.

In a mega-corporation, on the other hand, you can only see the area in which you're involved. The "big picture" is just too big for anyone (especially a young manager) to drink it all in.

I love the spirit and the energy you find in small businesses.

From 1989–1995, I served as the Chairman of The Ben Craig Center, a nonprofit small-business incubator affiliated with the University of North Carolina at Charlotte. (The Center is named after the late president of First Union, a bank with headquarters in Charlotte.) The Ben Craig Center offers budding young companies access to experienced business advisors, great business contacts, shared office services, and prime office space.

Entrepreneurs must make an investment to gain access to the Center's resources. Companies that take space at the Center pay rent just a bit below market prices. And all clients of the Center pay a monthly retainer fee. But it is clearly a sound investment. Since 1986, more than 80 companies—most with annual revenues from $10,000 to about $3,000,000—have tapped into the expertise and services offered by The Ben Craig Center. More than 80 percent of those businesses are still in operation.

I want to tell you, the people who launch these businesses have no trouble getting themselves out of bed in the morning. They have enormous energy and great faith in themselves and in their ideas. It takes guts to start up your own digital optics company, launch a trade paper for the construction industry, or form a private phone company that lets prison inmates place collect calls from confinement. Yet the entrepreneurs I met at the Center were also consistently open to new points of view. They lacked the shell of arrogance that encases so many hard chargers in major corporations.

Can people who work in a big company maintain the spirit, drive, and openness to new ideas you usually find only in an entrepreneurial start-up? It can be done. You just have to pursue the virtues of smallness, starting from the top of the business on down.

—■■■—

WHAT MAKES NUCOR'S headquarters so impressive, I think, is that it is so *un*impressive—twelve thousand square feet of rented office space in a Charlotte office park. We never got around to building an elaborate temple to ourselves, like those you see sprawled across swanky suburban enclaves. We're too busy building our *business*. Besides, our entire headquarters staff, including the clerical personnel, numbers just twenty-two.

The Virtues of Smallness

I take pride in Nucor's little headquarters. To me, a big headquarters isn't grand. It is a waste of money— a gross tribute to some executive's ego.

Worse still, ideas or initiatives originating in so wondrous a place as headquarters soon take on a special cache, despite the fact that the headquarters types who dreamt up the latest marketing strategy or new policy are often in the worst possible position to know what the business really needs. People out in the operating divisions receive the offerings from on high and say: "But, no one *asked* for this. Why is it here?" No wonder the standing joke among so many operations types is: " 'I'm from headquarters. I'm here to help!' "

In many corporations, the operating divisions not only have to endure ongoing absurdities from headquarters, they have to *pay* for them. There is no good way to allocate corporate expenses. Typically, corporations allocate their headquarters expenses to their operating divisions on the basis of sales, assets, or number of people, all of which are arbitrary. I never knew a division that felt its allocation was just. The only one who could allocate corporate expenses wisely is God, and I don't know what kind of job even He could do.

Our solution? Don't allocate any corporate expenses. And keep our headquarters so small, the expense is not much of an issue.

I'll admit, though, that you can't judge a business by its headquarters. To know a company, you have to know its people. In this crucial area, as in so many others, business decision makers consistently overlook the virtues of smallness—in this case, of small towns.

The traditional assumption is that you must locate a business in or near a big city. I suppose it was once necessary for major businesses to be in centers of commerce, transportation, and finance. Many also needed ready access to large pools of labor. From those legitimate needs sprang the enduring notion that, for a business to be big-league, it must be located in or near a big-league city.

We prefer small towns. We moved Nucor's headquarters from Phoenix, Arizona, to Charlotte, North Carolina, in 1966 when Charlotte was still much more a town than a city. And we've placed our divisions in such out-of-the way places as Jewett, Texas; Plymouth, Utah; Saint Joe, Indiana; Fort Payne, Alabama; and Hickman, Arkansas.

Nucor lore holds that I would fly into a city, rent a car, tune in a strong radio station, then drive out of town until the radio signal disappeared. And that would be the site of the next Nucor plant. It's not true, but if that had been our method of choosing where to locate Nucor businesses, we might well have ended up in many of the same places.

Labor in rural areas is a great untapped resource. I may be in a better position to appreciate that fact than are a lot of managers, because I have a natural affinity for country folks and for farmers, in particular. My mother came from a big farming family that settled the countryside outside Chicago before there even *was* a Chicago. She and Dad raised me in nearby Downers Grove, Illinois, so we often visited her family at the farm. And Downers Grove itself was essentially still a farm community.

Many Nucor divisions are surrounded by working fields, and many Nucor employees are from farming backgrounds. Of course, not all Nucor employees come from farming backgrounds or even from small towns. Quite a few come to us from the cities. When we opened our mill in Jewett, Texas, for example, we received hundreds of job applications from people in Houston and Dallas who wanted to move to a rural area. I'm glad we did. Jewett's population was just 425 at the time!

Whether they come to us from the country or the city, most people who stick with Nucor share values which I associate with rural America. Situating our businesses in small-town locales reinforces those values.

Our employees take great pride, for example, in being able to fix or make most things without help from anyone, a trait consistent with a stark reality of farm life: There is no shortage of things that break down, and very few repairmen or repair shops in the vicinity.

Wayne Hunt, shipping manager at Nucor-Yamato in Blytheville, Arkansas, is a case in point. Wayne's no farmer. He ran a trucking outfit for a while and has owned a gas station. But he sure knows how to fix things in a pinch. He demonstrated that a couple of springs ago, when the Mississippi floods inundated the barge port from which roughly one-third of Nucor-Yamato's product is shipped. "I got a call from John Correnti," Wayne recalls. "He said, 'Wayne, what's going on down there?' So I told him, 'The river's just swallowed up our port.' "

"But I shouldn't have been worried," Wayne continues, "because John had a suggestion for me. He said, 'Well then, I guess it's time for you to get creative. I'll call you tomorrow.' "

Wayne tells the story with a smile. He knows that responsibility and self-reliance go hand-in-hand with freedom, and Wayne (like most people at Nucor) values freedom. After John's call, Wayne gathered up a crew and rustled together some equipment. Remarkably, within a few days, they'd pumped out the port and built earthen dikes to hold out the surging river, and Nucor-Yamato was once again shipping steel by barge.

People in rural areas grow up learning lots of things on their own. We look for self-starters at Nucor. Johnny Dawkins, who sits at the controls of Nucor-Yamato's state-of-the-art rolling mill, is a good example. Johnny came to work for Nucor-Yamato as a production worker ten years ago, after working for a contractor that helped build our two

Arkansas facilities. A couple of Johnny's brothers work for Nucor, as well.

"I learned my job just by being here, basically," Johnny says as he eyes a deck of computer monitors in the control room overlooking Nucor-Yamato's Rolling Mill #2. "When these computers came in, we relied mostly on the pamphlets from the computer company. We'd get one computer up and running, figure out how it works, then move on to something else. The things we couldn't figure out, we'd put to the side until we could get someone to help us. Some folks from Nucor in Utah were a real big help, but mostly it was a process of trial and error."

Our spirit of self-reliance extends up to senior management, too. I prepare Nucor's annual report each year with Sam Siegel, our CFO, and Terry Lisenby, our controller. The three of us get together over a weekend to do a job most Fortune 500 companies hire an army of marketing staff and consultants to complete. Of course, we keep our annual report small—about twenty pages.

Another key difference between Nucor and most Fortune 500 companies is that we're not hung up on recruiting from big, prestigious universities. The typical big company wants to stock its management ranks with graduates from the biggest and most prestigious schools. But many of Nucor's managers and supervisors graduated from relatively small and lesser-known colleges or state schools. (A few never even went to college.) But they're all smart, down-to-earth, and ambitious. I wouldn't trade them for any management team in the world.

All in all, I'd say Nucor is a living testament to the fact that bigger isn't better. It's *different.* We've proven that a business with executives, managers, and people who embody the virtues of smallness and who sustain the spirit of a small company can compete with anyone. You'd better bring more than bigness if you want to scare us off.

—■■■—

CAN A COMPANY that's already big, in fact and in spirit, regain the virtues of smallness? Perhaps. But it will face significant obstacles.

One of the biggest is structure. In *The Practice of Management*, Peter Drucker wrote that "A company is as large as the management structure it requires," and that "In practice, any business that needs more than six or seven levels between rank-and-file employee and top management is too big."[1] If Drucker was right, think of the possibilities! Hypothetically, a business could grow ten-, twenty-, or fifty-fold in terms of revenues and still retain its small company character! All it would have to do is limit the number of its management levels. This is precisely what we've set out to do at Nucor, which is approaching

$4 billion in annual revenues with just four layers of management.

Fortune 500 executives visiting Nucor are intrigued to find that a major business can be so lean, simple, and rational—in other words, so much like a small business. But then they ask: "How do I cut management layers out of our company? How do we get from where *we* are to where *you* are?"

I can sympathize with any CEO who is faced with that challenge. In fact, whenever someone asks me, "If you were put in charge of US Steel, what would you do?," I answer, "I'd put a bullet in my head." I wouldn't, really, although it would likely prove a less agonizing fate. I suppose the best approach would be to plan the minimum number of layers, then move to that leaner structure as quickly as possible. I wouldn't wait for people to retire. If it has to be done, it's best to quickly get the pain out of the way.

A similar day of reckoning seems to be at hand for the federal government. We've heard plenty of bold pronouncements that "the era of big government is over." Where those pronouncements will lead remains to be seen. I do remember, though, talking with then-Governor Clinton in his state house office sometime in the mid-1980s. Nucor had decided to locate a second division in Arkansas. This pleased the Governor, as he was committed to building up his state's business infrastructure. When I told him about our determination to keep Nucor's operations small, simple, and free of red tape, even as our company continues to grow and to take on bigger and bigger challenges, his expression turned wistful. "Ken, you are lucky," Governor Clinton said. "When you decide that something ought to be done, it gets done. Bureaucracies are hard to work with. I wish we could be more like Nucor."

Some would contend that, in launching its Saturn Division, General Motors showed the world a practical and relatively pain-free path from bigness and bureaucracy to the virtues of smallness. But I see the launch of Saturn more as a concession than a victory. There was no way to make GM run like a small business, so they built a small business from the ground up, in Tennessee rather than in Michigan, taking great care to insulate Saturn from the taint of its bureaucratic big brother. As I understand it, very few people from GM were even offered the chance to go work for Saturn.

I can see why. It's not easy to change people. We've had a number of people come to Nucor from big steel companies. Some have thrived. John Correnti, our CEO, joined us out of US Steel fairly early in his career. But for most who try to cross that line—especially if they attempt it later in their careers—the transition is just too hard.

One of the toughest adjustments they face, Mike Parrish, our general manager in Hickman, has told me, is the transition from formality to informality. "We're a very ad hoc company," Mike says. "I've had managers come to work here who say, 'I'd like to see your quality program.' So I'll say, 'You mean, like a book?' And they'll say, 'Well, yeah.' So I have to tell them, 'Sorry, we're not big on programs of any kind. If we see something that needs improving, we just improve it.' Then they'll ask to look over our job descriptions, and I'll tell them, 'Job descriptions are pretty much the same for everyone here: "Come to work and be productive as heck for twelve hours." ' Then, if they still haven't caught on, they'll want to review all our policies, so they can do a good job of 'enforcing compliance.' So I have to tell them, 'We're not big on policies, either.' "

Another tough adjustment for refugees from big steel is the transition from tight control to lots of freedom. All the boundaries they knew are gone. They see a department manager crawling around to rebrick a furnace, or a production worker debating with an engineer, or a team of employees purchasing new equipment, and they don't know *what* to think.

The greatest transition of all, though, is learning how to communicate all the time, with everyone. That's what people in small businesses do. In fact, communication is probably the single greatest virtue of smallness. By limiting the number of employees in each division to four or five hundred, we give our managers the chance to maintain personal, face-to-face communications with the people who make the business go. We haven't fired many managers from Nucor, but 90 percent of those who have been dismissed were let go because they failed to communicate with employees.

All of our managers spend a great deal of their time talking with their people. "I sit down with every new employee within a week or two of them coming to work here," reports Dan DiMicco, general manager of Nucor-Yamato. "We usually talk for a few hours, and I've had more than five hundred such conversations since 1991. The whole idea is to start the communication. We usually find that we have a lot in common, but we also learn about our differences, and those are valuable. It's like on a football team—you don't want all your players to be the same size or have the same skills. You need a variety of people who can do a variety of things, and you have to help them all blend into a winner. That begins with communication."

———■■■———

THE NOTION THAT "bigger is better" is ubiquitous in business thinking, yet so implicit, we rarely give it notice. It is the natural product of the consolidation of enterprise into larger and larger units, culminating in the highly successful and awesomely powerful mega-corporation. Bigger *works* in business. But smaller works, too.

Big businesses longing to act more like small ones will have to face up to a harsh truth: There is no shortcut from big and bureaucratic to small and nimble. Big, bureaucratic companies cannot truly change until executives, managers, and employees alike embrace the virtues of smallness.

7

RISKS AND ADVENTURES

B Y THE SPRING of 1954, I had left International
Harvester to join Illium Corporation in Freeport,
Illinois, where I was manager of production and chief
engineer. My new domain was a foundry housed
in a five-car garage. The concrete floor bore count-
less scars from molten metal. I often had to crawl
around inside our antiquated direct-arc melting
furnace, which would cover me in dust. My finger-
nails were blackened with grime. I really liked this
place!

I knocked twice and let myself into the office
where Ken Burgess, the president of the company,

sat sifting through invoices, purchase orders, and production reports.

"What's on your mind?" Ken asked.

"We need a machine to produce pipe."

"Costs too much," Ken said, not bothering to look up from his paperwork. We'd covered this ground before. It was getting old.

"I know." The price tag of the machine I wanted was about $250,000, roughly $245,000 more than the company could raise. "But I thought maybe we could build our own pipe machine."

Now he looked up. "We can do that?"

"I'd like to try." I shared my idea for making a pipe casting machine using a large sand-lined pipe set on rollers that would spin 600–700 revolutions per minute. Ken asked a few questions, then gave me the go-ahead to build it, with a budget not to exceed $5,000.

Building a pipe machine was a welcome diversion from the foundrymen's routine. Within a few months, we had engineered a homemade machine for casting pipe. Total cost, about $5,000.

Of course, it lacked some of the refinements you'd find in the "store-bought" variety. It wasn't pretty. And every time we turned it on, it screeched like a freight train braking its way down a mountain.

That was a problem. None of the foundrymen would go near the contraption. We had our pipe machine, but we still weren't making pipe.

I went to Ken's office. "I need you to come and help me pour the first melt into the pipe machine," I told him.

"Why?"

"The men don't trust it. We have to pour a melt to show them that it will work, and I can't do it by myself."

Ken got up, grim-faced, and followed me back into the foundry. Most of our fifty employees gathered around to watch us. I like to think they wished us success, but their fascination was probably more akin to a crowd gathering below a man teetering on a window ledge.

We poured the melt out of the furnace into a two-man ladle, carried it up to the pouring stand, took a deep breath, and poured the melt into the pipe machine. No problem! It worked perfectly! Well, I guess we'd made our point. The foundrymen went to work making pipe. Ken clapped me on the back. We were in the pipe business!

A few months later, Ken had Illium's board of directors down from Chicago to witness this magnificent product of our ingenuity. Unfortunately, one of the baked sand dams broke during the demonstration and shot a ten-foot pinwheel of molten metal out through the garage wall like a buzz saw going through butter, cutting the building in half. Fortunately, no one was hurt. I learned that day that even a board of directors can be compelled to run very, very fast.

—■■■—

SOME PEOPLE WOULD count such an episode as a failure, I suppose, but I don't, because the machine did work. We *did* build it and it *did* run profitably, if only for a while. With just $5,000 and our collective brain power, we created a machine that did many of the same things as one that cost $250,000. I've since made it a point never to underestimate what small groups of people can accomplish, even with the barest of resources.

Of course, people won't *try* to accomplish extra-ordinary things if their managers won't tolerate failure. You should take care to never criticize when things turn out badly. That's a surefire way to stop people from taking prudent risks. As the manager of people who made decisions that turned out badly, remember you were the one who allowed them to fail. So if you must dish out blame, give yourself a good helping first. That often curbs the urge.

Once the impulse to criticize is expunged from your system, you can study the experience with those who went through it. Help your people avoid making the same mistake again. Figure out together if the idea is worth attempting another time and, if it is, what adjustments should be made in the approach. Don't wallow in the failure. Learn from it. Look forward, not back. Urge them to try again.

You should also try to be genuinely open to the ideas people bring to you. Even well-intentioned managers may slip almost automatically into evaluating or criticizing the ideas others share with them. Yet I've found the only sure way to show people you're receptive to their ideas is to say nothing but "OK, do it," or "OK, I'll help."

Remember, you'll never know how good an idea is until somebody tries it. And even if the idea fails, the *experience* of trying it will contribute to the success of the business and its people over the long term.

Personally, I can't stand it when there are no strange new ideas floating around the company. Whenever that happens, I launch a few ideas of my own, then start nagging people to help me test them out. It works every time, because most people would rather pursue their *own* ideas than those you push at them.

— ■ ■ ■ —

THE MANAGEMENT mind-set that promotes innovation and risk-taking is rooted in a philosophy, or perhaps it is merely an attitude: Life is an adventure! Crazy things happen! We come into this world with a severe bump. I don't know why some people expect the rest of the ride to be smooth.

Fortunately, even life's minor catastrophes can make you a better person. As a teenager, I was driving my father's Studebaker home from a party at which we'd made peanut brittle. The suspension in Dad's Studebaker wasn't very forgiving, and neither were the country roads in Downers Grove, Illinois. One particularly big chuckhole sent a jar of syrup, left over from the candy making, onto the floor by the front seat. Reflexively, I touched the brakes, and that syrup jar rolled flush onto the gas pedal. The sudden acceleration shot the Studebaker straight into a stout old oak. I escaped with minor bruises, and the tree seemed no worse for wear, but Dad's Studebaker was a goner.

Or so I thought. My father arrived at the scene shortly after the police did. It was 2 a.m. I was sitting on the crumpled Studebaker's running board with my head in my hands. "Are you okay?" Dad asked. I told him that my chest hurt, but I thought I'd be alright. "That will teach you to fight with trees," he said. I ventured a nervous laugh. Good one, Dad. Was that it? Was that all he had to say? I should be so lucky. "You're going to fix this car," he told me.

Fix it? Did he know what he was asking?

He sure did. In fact, he helped me through most of it. Straightening the car's bent-up frame. Replacing smashed parts. Hammering out dents. I took the engine out, ground the valves, and put new pistons in. It took more than a year of serious effort to get that car back on the road. Many days, I just wanted to quit, but Dad wouldn't let me. He'd just use those times to remind me: "Much good work is lost for the lack of a little more," which was one of his favorite sayings. When we finally got his Studebaker in running condition, Dad made it mine. I owned a car! Even better, I knew how to build a car pretty much from the ground up.

Experiences like that convinced me not to fear making mistakes. I have no desire to be perfect. In fact, none of the people I've seen do impressive things in life are perfect. They never settle for latching onto one approach or mastering one way of doing things. They experiment. And they often fail. But they gain something significant from every failure. That's what it takes to achieve, I think, in business as well as in life.

———■■■———

We have a saying at Nucor: "If it's worth doing, it's worth doing poorly." It means don't study an idea to death with experts and committees. Get on with it and see if it works.

This approach leads to more than a few failures. Probably half of the new technologies, approaches, and other ideas we try fail. Every Nucor plant has its little storehouse of equipment that was bought, tried, and discarded. We think some mistakes are perfectly acceptable. The knowledge we gather from our so-called "failures" may lead us to spectacular success.

Nucor's most heralded success was our leap into the flat-rolled steel business, which we accomplished in 1989 by gambling on a highly experimental process called "thin-slab casting." It was a bet many thought we would lose. Bethlehem Steel even circulated a report detailing why we would fail.

Much that has been written about this episode—the decision to go with thin-slab casting and the building of our revolutionary new steel mill in Craw-fordsville, Indiana—is at least a little misleading. Many accounts imply that we threw all caution to the wind, or that we were heroically courageous. We didn't, and we weren't. Some risks, even big ones, are worth taking once you've weighed them against appropriate criteria.

Before we bet on thin-slab casting, we assessed the new technology's potential to improve Nucor's strategic position, the magnitude and durability of the competitive advantage we might realize, and the likelihood that our company could make this un-tested method of producing steel commercially viable. We had followed the development of thin-slab casting throughout the decade. We looked before we leaped.

Why were we looking at thin-slab casting? Through most of the 1980s, Nucor's strategic posi-tion was severely limited. You might even say we were trapped inside a box. Our mini-mills proved remarkably efficient producers of steel bars, beams, and angles. But the market for those products accounts for little more than a third of the total market for steel. That was our box.

Outside our box was the market for flat-rolled steel, which is used in construction as well as in making pipe, farm machinery, automobiles, and appliances. Flat-rolled accounts for more than half of all the steel sold in the U.S. If we were going to grow Nucor to its full potential, we needed to sell flat-rolled steel.

The problem was, Nucor couldn't *make* flat-rolled steel. Why? Before 1989, the only kind of facility that could turn out flat-rolled steel was an integrated steel mill. "Integrated" refers to mills which process a raw material, iron ore, all the way through to a finished product. Nucor's mini-mills, in contrast, are essentially recyclers. Our "raw material" is scrap metal.

The integrated steel-making process is very complex and the facilities required to carry it out are massive. A typical integrated mill employs more than 3,000 people and produces three million or more tons of steel annually. One key step in the traditional method of making flat-rolled steel is turning ten-inch-thick "slabs" of steel into flat rolls a fraction of an inch thick. In fact, this step alone entails cooling the slab, reheating it, sending it through a breakdown mill, and then on through a finishing mill. The mills required to do the job sometimes stretch out for more than a mile. There was no way Nucor would be comfortable operating a facility that large. Nor could we garner the capital required to build it. We'd have to find another way out of our box.

Our best hope was a new technology called "thin-slab casting." As the name implies, thin-slab casting would turn freshly melted steel into a much thinner slab, just two inches thick. For obvious reasons, a two-inch slab could be turned into flat-rolled with far less rolling equipment than could the ten-inch slabs that are cast in the integrated mills. In fact, the process would be "continuous." A thin slab would be sent immediately into a finishing mill, while it was still hot, eliminating the need for massive rolling facilities. The job might even be done in the relatively inexpensive confines of a mini-mill.

There was a reason, of course, why thin-slab casting was still a theory rather than an option. It is very difficult to move molten metal into a two-inch mold with speed. The entire process would have to be much more precise.

We found that out for ourselves. As early as 1980, we experimented with a belt-driven thin-slab caster. It proved to be yet another of our multimillion-dollar "failures." The belt caster created thin slabs, but the pouring system required was complicated and expensive. We heard that a few Japanese firms were also experimenting with thin-slab casters, apparently with little success.

The breakthrough came from a West German equipment maker called SMS Schloemann-Siemag. We'd been following their efforts. We even took a trip to their factory in 1984 to discuss their thin-slab casting concept—a funnel-shaped mold with a nozzle that would allow precision control of the flow of molten metal inside the caster. In their 1986 demonstration, SMS produced a continuous two-inch slab about thirty feet long. They were getting close.

In 1987, SMS called to say they had perfected what they thought was a commercially applicable thin-slab casting process. SMS approached us first, they admitted, because they didn't think anyone else would attempt a full-scale implementation of their technology. They may have been right. Financially, the big steel companies could more readily afford to risk the investment than could Nucor, but they had been making flat-rolled steel from ten-inch slabs for so long, it was hard for them to envision any other method of production.

We, on the other hand, were intrigued. This could be the breakthrough that would help Nucor step out of its box and into the flat-rolled steel business.

Nucor could build a thin-slab mill at a fraction of the cost of building an integrated mill. So we'd have a huge competitive advantage in terms of capital costs. We also anticipated that thin-slab casting would be a far more cost-effective *ongoing* operation than the complex, stop-and-go approach the integrated mills used. We projected a cost advantage of up to $50 per ton over competing grades of flat-rolled product.

Best of all, it would take a long time for competitors to match our technology. Big steel was unlikely to even try thin-slab casting. They had far too much invested—emotionally and in terms of capital—in traditional steel making. And few of our competitors had been researching thin-slab processes to the extent we had. They'd face a steep learning curve. Our competitive advantage would likely be durable as well as sizable.

History, by the way, has shown these assumptions to be correct. Our mills now turn out flat-rolled steel with a labor input of just 0.6 man-hours per ton, compared with 3–4 man-hours per ton at the best of the world's big steel companies. We're often able to price our products $50–$75 per ton below what big steel competitors charge. And nearly seven years passed before the first competitive facility used continuous, thin-slab casting to make flat-rolled steel.

In 1987, however, all the tantalizing possibilities still rested on the answer to one very dicey question: Could Nucor make thin-slab casting work?

We thought we could. Nucor, after all, was a metallurgical company with twenty years experience making steel products. We had a track record of successfully implementing innovations, most notably the mini-mill. Thin-slab casting was, in some ways, a comparable challenge. Nucor might be a poor choice to stage a new ballet or market a new kind of insurance, but give us our due—we were a great candidate to take thin-slab casting from experimental potential to commercial reality. If anyone could do it, Nucor could.

Brave talk, especially considering the size of the lump in my throat. Steel making is a cyclical business—a business of booms and busts. Supermarkets offer a classic contrast. People have to buy groceries every week, even when the economy is down. Since grocery store revenues experience relatively mild fluctuations, supermarkets can risk carrying substantial debt most of the time. On the other hand, people can go months or years without steel. Sink a steel company too deep into debt before the industry plunges into a long "bust" cycle, and you may not come out the other side, especially if the technology you invest in flops.

At the very least, heavy debt increases interest expenses and the chances you'll have to lay people off. That's a risk Nucor does not take lightly. We have a history of conservative financing, so we won't be too vulnerable to down cycles. We try to keep our debt below 30 percent of total capital. Most years it does not exceed 10 percent. However, the investment required to acquire and apply thin-slab casting technology would push our capital resources to the limit. If *this* roll of the dice came up snake eyes, there would be plenty of pain to share.

Three of us from Nucor—Dave Aycock (then our president), a Nucor engineer, and myself—sat down with four principals from SMS, starting on a Thursday. By Sunday night, we'd purchased a thin-slab caster and a rolling mill. We'd committed the company to a total outlay of more than $200 million, all riding on a technology that no one could say, for certain, would actually work.

I sure hoped we were doing the right thing. All the while we were building the new thin-slab mill at Crawfordsville, people would ask me: "Are you worried, Ken?," and I'd say, "I sleep like a baby . . . I wake up every two hours and cry!"

Thanks to the superb efforts of more people than can ever be properly acknowledged here, Crawfordsville was and is a commercial success. We broke out of our box and into the flat-rolled steel business. Nucor has since built two more mini-mills that produce flat-rolled steel using thin-slab casting—the Hickman mill in 1992 and our newest mill in Berkeley, South Carolina, which came on line in 1997. Our company has grown into the third-largest steel maker in America.

What lessons can be drawn from Nucor's decision to gamble on thin-slab casting? The most important one, I think, is that you should never let someone else—even a so-called expert—tell you if a risk is worth taking. You have to decide that for yourself. In 1987, about the only people who felt confident our big gamble would pay off was us. Most informed observers in the industry thought it was just too much of a stretch. But then, we were the only people in a position to accurately gauge our chances of success.

Here's another lesson: Don't fall into the trap of ruling out failure. Risk, by definition, carries the possibility of failure. See that possibility. Study it, but never, ever hide from it.

—■■■—

OUR NEW MILLS incorporate significant refinements over Crawfordsville, and so our thin-slab casting technology remains on the leading edge. But we suffer no illusions that thin-slab casting will be a leading-edge technology for long. In fact, I'll be very disappointed if it is, because we're still out there pushing the edge.

In 1994, Nucor broke ground for the first plant ever designed to commercially produce iron carbide—fine black particles of iron processed out of iron ore. Why does Nucor make iron carbide? The single largest expense in operating our mini-mills is the cost of scrap metal—especially high-quality scrap—a commodity for which prices may fluctuate widely. We were searching for ways to reduce our reliance on scrap as a raw material, and thereby stabilize our costs.

Over the course of a year, we tested every commercially available scrap substitute, then chose to make iron carbide. It was potentially the most cost-efficient option, and it was a good match to our steel making process. Iron carbide is easy to handle. The fine particles can be blown directly into our furnaces, where they mix into the molten metal faster than sugar dissolves into tea. The carbon in iron carbide is also a fuel that helps heat the melt. Our tests showed that iron carbide could be substituted for at least a fifth, and perhaps as much as one-half, of the scrap metal used in making our steel.

The question was, could we produce large volumes of the stuff at a cost significantly below the price of high-quality scrap metal? No one had done it before and, if we failed, the whole exercise would be a monumental waste of time and money. We decided to go for it.

Most observers assumed we'd begin by building a small demonstration facility to prove the iron carbide process. That is how chemical companies typically proceed. But that's not our way. Remember, we think that "If it's worth doing, it's worth doing poorly." So we proceeded straight to constructing a full-scale facility. Total cost, about $80 million. When the press asked if our iron carbide process would work, I admitted: "It's hard to know. It's really a giant laboratory experiment."

We decided to build our iron carbide plant in Trinidad. Nucor had never built an offshore facility before. But all the necessary ingredients were there: a ready supply of iron ore (from Brazil), plenty of natural gas to heat the ore and provide hydrogen and methane, and a favorable business environment. The government of Trinidad welcomed us to their Point Lisas Industrial Estate, which has room for us to build more iron carbide plants in the future. Logistics of transportation were also favorable. We could ship the finished product to New Orleans, then carry it on barges up the Mississippi to our mini-mills in Hickman, Arkansas, and Crawfordsville, Indiana.

The Trinidad plant was up and running by early 1995 but our people down there encountered plenty of problems. One snafu involved mechanisms called heat exchangers. The folks who did the original design engineering for us recommended that we use a shell-and-tube design, but we chose to go with a plate-and-fin design instead, based on cost differentials and other analyses. Well, the heat exchangers we chose kept clogging up, which slowed the whole manufacturing process to a crawl.

OK, it was time to admit it. Our judgment was wrong. The engineering firm had been right. We pulled out the heat exchangers we'd selected and replaced them with the type originally recommended by the design engineers, a step that cost us more than $5 million and set us back more than six months. That didn't make any of us happy, but it's the kind of thing that happens when you try something completely new. There was no sense getting discouraged.

We knew it was going to be rough. But we figured that with the right kind of support, in the right kind of environment, our people would find a way to make it work.

They're doing just that. Production is steadily increasing, we're producing a better-quality product, and our costs per ton are declining steadily as our people debug and modify the operation. We also believe a new hydrogen generator may enable us to increase production to a level much closer to designed capacity while maintaining high product quality. Our goal is to produce a product that could revolutionize the economics of making steel from scrap metal.

The possibilities of iron carbide are wondrous. In theory, the 6 percent carbon content within iron carbide could provide most and perhaps all of the energy needed to make steel. Iron carbide could therefore enable us to make steel without the need for ore, coke, blast furnaces, scrap metal, or electricity. All it would take is iron carbide and oxygen. Such a process would be environmentally clean and would produce steel of remarkable purity.

Of course, at this point, there is no such process. And no one can say for sure that we'll find a way to do it. But then, it wasn't so long ago that they were saying the same thing about thin-slab casting and the commercial production of iron carbide.

—■■■—

THERE'S A CORRELATION, I believe, between age and one's readiness to take risks. That's no great revelation. It's human nature to become more circumspect with experience and to grow more cautious when we have more to lose. The more success we achieve in life, the greater the temptation to rest on our laurels.

I'm still the same person. But I've noticed myself growing a bit less comfortable with risk and a bit less inclined to be aggressive. I find myself compensating for an inclination to play it safe.

It's a good thing I am, too, because the last thing I want to do is play it safe. Aversion to risk is deadly in business, especially in industries marked by rapid advances in technology. And, these days, what industry doesn't fall into that category?

The more senior the manager, of course, the more crucial it is for him to encourage innovation and risk-taking in others. I think most senior managers are aware of this responsibility. What they may not be aware of, though, is that they may themselves be growing less tolerant of risks.

Allowing for that very possibility, I have become a more conscious and explicit champion of taking *good* risks as I've advanced to more senior positions in management. I now work to manage in ways that I once pursued with less forethought. But they are the *same* behaviors, and they are behaviors I believe are appropriate for managers at all stages of their careers.

—■-■-■—

MANAGERS WHO AVOID risk and fear failure spend their entire careers cheating themselves, their people, and their companies. They cut themselves off from their greatest opportunities to achieve. They deny their people the chance to grow. And they doom their businesses to perform at levels below their true potential.

If you're taking as many risks as a good manager should, you *will* fail. That's just the price you pay to play the game. You must look failure in the eye.

Of course, you don't want to fail *too* often. To determine which risks are worth taking and which are better left alone, you have to know more than the facts. You have to know yourself. You have to realize that your fears and ambitions are the lenses through which you view and assess risks, and that the image those lenses convey may not always be true. Take time to factor yourself—where you are in your career and how that may influence your thinking—into the equation before you decide where and when to place your bets.

But *do* place them, even though you know you could lose. And once the chips are down, don't think about failing. Think about winning.

8

Ethics over Politics

"ethics: a standard of conduct and moral judgment."
—*Webster's Dictionary*

W HILE I WAS still in my 20s, working for a small company, my boss came into my office one day and said, "I think I want to call a lawyer."

"What's the problem?" I asked.

"Somebody tested positive for silicosis."

Silicosis is a serious illness caused by the buildup of silicon particles in the lungs. At that time, silicosis was not uncommon among mold workers in foundries, so we screened for the condition regularly.

"So why do you need a lawyer?" I asked.

"The guy who tested positive quit last week to take a job with another foundry," my boss said. "I want to see if I'm still legally required to tell him that he tested positive."

I could hardly believe my ears. In fact, I blew my stack. "You don't need to talk to any lawyer! This is simple. You've got to tell the man that he is sick!"

Well, I guess my yelling and banging on the table stunned my boss into realizing that what he was doing was absolutely unacceptable. He had a moral obligation to let that man know he had contracted silicosis. He immediately informed the man of the test result.

You can't put your ethics in your pocket when you become a businessperson. If something is wrong outside the realm of business, then it's wrong inside the realm of business.

I'm proudest of my colleagues in those times when their ethics come to the fore. One time, for example, a Nucor-Vulcraft sales manager attended a meeting of joist industry executives in Washington, D.C. Before dinner, someone in the group suggested that the gathering presented "a good opportunity to work on stabilizing our prices." That was a code for fixing prices—which is illegal—and everyone knew it.

Our sales manager picked up his glass of scotch and turned it over onto the table. Then he walked out the door.

Of course, ethics in business are not always clear cut. In some ways, business resembles war. It is quite acceptable for one business to intentionally destroy another, as long as it uses acceptable weapons—superior products, cost-efficiency, honest marketing—to do so. Where do you draw the line when it's *your* business under attack? How far can you ethically go to protect the livelihoods of people you care about? Chances are, you'd go further when your business is seriously threatened than when it seems secure.

What's more, generally accepted standards of what is ethical in business are continually changing. Monopolies, for example, were once an accepted form of business organization. Now they are illegal, in most instances. So is the once-common practice of "insider trading" of stocks. Similarly, the standards for what constitutes truth in advertising are more stringent than they once were. And the drive to ensure equal opportunity has revolutionized what constitutes ethical practices in hiring, firing, and advancement.

Your personal standards can also change. Some things you might consider wrong today may have seemed perfectly fine to you in the past.

In the early 1950s, I was chief metallurgist and sales manager at Cannon-Muskegon Corporation, a small plant set in the Muskegon sand dunes along Lake Michigan. The job was a metallurgist's dream. We made a variety of nickel- and cobalt-base alloys and cast them to exacting requirements, primarily for use in building aircraft.

But I was particularly excited when the Nuclear Energy Group of Westinghouse asked Cannon-Muskegon to cast a uranium ingot to be extruded into the fuel rods for the world's first nuclear submarine, the U.S.S. *Nautilus*.

The schedule was tight. Westinghouse wanted us to deliver the ingot within two weeks. No later. So we went on alternating shifts of twelve hours, melting uranium in a vacuum furnace around the clock. Finally, on a Sunday morning we cast the ingot. It was four inches round, a foot long, and weighed about 75 pounds.

The problem was, we were flat out of time and, on a Sunday morning, we couldn't get anyone to ship the ingot to the Westinghouse engineers. We decided to take it ourselves.

Two of us went to the Muskegon Airport and bought tickets for the Chicago flight. We put the ingot on the scale where they weighed the luggage. "What is it?" the airline agent asked. "Uranium," we replied. "You can't bring uranium on a plane!" we were told.

We jumped back into the car, drove to Grand Rapids, and booked ourselves onto their next flight to Chicago. When the airline agent there asked us what we were carrying, I said, "An iron ingot." He waved us on board.

Let's look at the facts:

1. We lied to the airline agent in Grand Rapids.

2. We violated the law.

3. The ingot posed no danger. You could have sat on that ingot for fifty years and not got any more exposure to radiation than you would living in Denver.

4. The Westinghouse people needed that ingot immediately to move ahead with a project considered vital to national defense, the building of the U.S. Navy's first nuclear submarine.

Was what we did unethical? I'll let you decide.

—◼◼◼—

OBVIOUSLY, YOU NEED to set down some ethical standards for your business in your policy book, so they are clearly stated and understood by everybody. Nucor's personnel policies include a brief section called "Standards of Business Conduct." It calls on all of us to strictly observe and comply with the law, to exercise the highest degree of honesty and integrity in all our dealings with others, and to avoid situations in which our personal interests might conflict with the interests of Nucor (e.g., no employee should borrow money or accept gifts from any person doing business or seeking to do business with the company).

Of course, no personnel policy ensures ethical behavior. There is no such thing as a fraud-proof business.

Quite recently, in fact, the controller of a Nucor division was found to have embezzled more than $400,000 from the company. Apparently he had a gambling problem and was desperate. After he resigned from the company, he considered moving to the mountains of western North Carolina and becoming a minister. Another fellow, a Nucor shipping manager who also owns a trucking firm, got caught invoicing the company for phantom freight charges which, over a ten-year period, totaled more than $750,000. The Internal Revenue Service caught him, along with us.

Those things will happen. There's not much you can do to prevent a manager from overriding your stated standards, beyond putting in appropriate checks and balances that make it hard for people to get away with lying, cheating, or stealing.

Nor can a policy encompass the full range of our ethical responsibilities. (I doubt that many of our employees, when faced with an ethical dilemma, consult their personnel manuals.) Many of the standards of conduct in a business come by way of example. Most people look to the actions of their fellow managers and employees to assess what is acceptable and moral conduct.

That's only natural. We all start to develop a sense of what is right or wrong early in life, usually by observing our parents. My father was never big on stating rules, but he was a highly principled man. Once, my older brother took coupons for a free ice cream cone from every newspaper in the neighborhood. I doubt any of our neighbors would have noticed or much cared. But when my brother showed the coupons to my father, Dad told him, "Take them all back." My brother had to knock on each door, explain that he'd taken the coupon, and return it. That made a big impression on us. It certainly left no doubt in our minds that taking something that doesn't belong to you—even a newspaper coupon—is wrong. Dad was a very consistent model of ethical behavior.

The examples set by those around us tell us a lot about what constitutes ethical behavior, but they can't tell us everything. Each day, we all face situations that require us to exercise our own moral judgment. As a practical matter, deciding what is ethical in business often boils down to finding the intersection of what is equitable, right, and practical. We want to do what is equitable and right because we strive to be ethical people and to treat one another fairly. We want to do what's practical because we're in business.

If you look hard enough, you can almost always find options that are equitable, right, *and* practical. It takes a bit more effort up front to find options that meet all three criteria, but in the long run it saves you a lot of headaches.

That was how we decided what to do, for example, when Ivory Herbert got arthritis. Ivory worked on the production line at Vulcraft making steel joists. He'd been doing heavy labor for us for more than twenty years. With the onset of the arthritis, he couldn't keep up that kind of effort, but Ivory said he wasn't ready to retire. So we trained Ivory, a sixty-year-old man, to operate a crane. Ivory became a good crane man and worked hard for another four or five years. He quit when he felt the time was right.

As far as I know, no one at Nucor questioned the decision to give Ivory the option to keep working in another capacity. Nobody complained that it deprived them of an opportunity or violated their rights, in some way. They saw it for what it was—the decent thing to do. It was also practical. Ivory carried his weight each and every day on the job. And it was equitable. We'd do the same for any employee, under similar circumstances.

Automation is another case in point. It hasn't posed much of a dilemma to us, although I know quite a few companies have been troubled by the tradeoff between technology and jobs. Most of the time, automation does eliminate jobs. The loss of those jobs, not automation itself, is why people tend to resist technological change. Our simple answer: When we automate a process, we guarantee every employee who is affected the opportunity to choose between two jobs that pay as much or more than the position they will lose.

I've also found that searching for the intersection of what is equitable, right, and practical is the best way to deal with the famous "Peter Principle," which holds that "in a hierarchy every employee tends to rise to the level of his incompetence."[1] You will surely confront the Peter Principle during your career as a manager, and it is among the toughest situations you will face.

When you find yourself managing someone who has been promoted to a level where he is incompetent in his job, you have three options: You can promote that person (to get him out of the way); move him sideways into some other job that you think he'll be better able to perform (we find that this works less than half the time); or you can fire him.

In my experience, the last option is usually the best thing for the company and for the employee. But you shouldn't fire him right away. Wait until it is absolutely clear to the employee himself and to everyone around him that he's not competent in the job. Then, when you let him go, everyone will ask, "Why didn't you let him go sooner?" The decision will be seen as equitable, right, and practical.

—■■■—

I'VE BEEN KNOWN to speak out against a wide range of practices that pass for "business as usual" in the world today. For the record, I firmly believe that businesses should keep themselves separate from politics and government, treat people equitably, and speak the plain truth. That's why I'm against:

- Corporations funding political candidates and PACs.

- Lobbyists. (Nucor has none.)

- Government regulations that are meaningless and serve only to restrict business.

- Government tariffs. I think industry has to stand on its own two feet against foreign competition.

- Subsidies for business in any form. The Department of Defense once gave $10 million to US Steel and Bethlehem Steel to experiment with thin-slab casting. Their conclusion? "It doesn't work." Then we came along with no government money and showed that it can.

- Mandatory retirement age. There are people who should retire in their 40s, and people who can work into their 80s.

- Discrimination. No one should be denied a job for which he or she is qualified.

- Financial reports that distort the earnings. After reading some annual reports, I feel like screaming: "WHAT IS THE INCOME OF THE COMPANY?!" They put so much corporate spin on the numbers, you can hardly tell.

You disagree? It's a free country.

—■■■—

THE WORLD OF business is loaded with temptations. There are so many ways to cut corners that seem to offer such easy roads to whatever you may want, your conscience can be overwhelmed by that mighty tag team, the ego and the id. In fact, all the primary rewards in business—prestige, power, money—appeal to our more base cravings. The whole system is designed to fuel the fires of temptation. And while there are many good people in business, there are precious few saints.

For all those reasons and more, behaving ethically in business can be very hard work. But it is work you *must* take on.

I'll be the first to admit that I've sometimes pushed the line to get what I want. But I will say this: I have never pretended that the line wasn't there.

9

THE BOTTOM LINE

MANY MANAGERS, I've found, struggle to accept the simplicity of Nucor. Even after we answer their questions about our company as completely and openly as we can, they often think that there must be something more . . . something we haven't told them about what makes us successful.

But the truth is, simplicity *is* what makes Nucor successful. At least, it's a big part of it. We've consciously tried to push aside the complexity, hierarchy, bureaucracy, and much of the other nonsense that characterizes life inside so many large corporations. Perhaps that is why this book, which presents all the main elements of Nucor's approach to business, isn't very long. We're easy to explain.

Mainly, we try to keep our focus on what really matters—bottom-line performance and long-term survival. That's what we want our people to be thinking about. Management takes care not to distract the company with a lot of talk about other issues. We don't clutter the picture with lofty vision statements, ask employees to pursue vague, intermediate objectives like "excellence," or burden them with complex business strategies. Our competitive strategy is to build manufacturing facilities economically, and to operate them efficiently. Period.

"Build facilities economically" distills our approach to capital investment. We start every steel-making operation off on a very cost-competitive footing. Building a mini-mill costs Nucor just $200 to $500 per ton of annual manufacturing capacity, as compared to $1,400 to $1,700 per ton to build traditional mills favored by integrated steel producers.

Then, by making low costs and high productivity ongoing priorities in the operation of our plants (i.e., operating them efficiently), we can extend that initial cost advantage and keep our costs continually in check. Basically, we ask our employees to produce more product for less money. Then we reward them for doing that well. Simple.

Keeping our business simple helps us to be unusually straightforward in our dealings with customers, as well. Our pricing policy is a good case in point. Nucor publishes its prices, like everyone else in the steel industry. But, *un*like most everyone else, the prices we publish for our steel products are the prices we charge. To everyone. No special discounts. No exceptions.

Why is that important? Over the years, we've heard from dozens of customers who've told us that discounting had a negative effect on their business. For example, the manager of a service center (a steel distributorship) in Iowa told me that he got burned when he bought a large order of steel from a big producer, paying a sum close to the published price. A week later, the same steelmaker sold a large order of the same product—at a very steep discount—to a steel broker who competed with the service center. For the next several months, the service center bumped into that broker on just about every bid. The service center manager was left with just two choices: *a*) match the broker's prices and lose money, or *b*) sit on the steel and make no money. He said he felt that the big steel producer had "betrayed" him and, in a sense, it had. By not offering discounts, Nucor treats all customers equally. We give them a level playing field. And we make dealing with us about as simple as a business transaction can be.

One of the great advantages of consistently doing just what you say you'll do is the credibility you gain with customers. Your salespeople don't have to dazzle anyone. All they have to do is present the facts.

In 1975, for example, we published this open letter in the industry trade journals.

Dear Steel Customers:

A number of larger steel companies have decided, almost simultaneously, to match Nucor's prices. You might ask how they intend to do this, since they do not have the same pricing structure. Obviously, they intend to match our prices on a customer-by-customer basis. (It is interesting to note that in most cases their reductions are only on the products and sizes made by Nucor.)

At Nucor, we place great emphasis on building mills economically and running them efficiently. I suggest you ask some of the larger producers if they can build plants, as we do, with a capital cost of under $90 per ton of annual capacity. Can they produce steel with less than 5 man-hours per ton? (If you count only our production workers, it's under 3.) Last year the seven largest steel companies in the United States had total employment costs that averaged more than $110 per ton. Ours were under $45. *Our* prices are based on these lower costs, and we operate profitably.

Chances are, our salesman won't call on you very often. He probably doesn't play golf. The odds are he won't take you to dinner. And I am sure he won't offer you a ride on his ore boat. But he will provide high-quality steel angles, rounds, channels, flats, special shapes and forging billets at economical prices. My only regret is that we don't make an even wider range of products and sizes so that even more steel customers could benefit from our efficiencies. I suggest you buy from Nucor if you want a lower price from the larger steel companies.

Sincerely,
F. Kenneth Iverson
President

I often say that employees are a lot smarter than most managers give them credit for being. Customers are smart, too. They know that, over the long term, a supplier can't continue to cut prices on products that do not make them money. To counter our competitors' pricing moves, all we had to do was tell the simple truth.

That's what John Correnti, Nucor's CEO, intends to do as vice chairman of the new Steel Alliance, a five-year, $100 million ad campaign touting steel. A reporter from *The Charlotte Observer* recently called

John and said, "Why did you choose to get involved in this mainstream campaign? Are Nucor's days as a maverick in the industry over? Does this represent a change in your philosophy?"

John's response ran in the next day's paper. "No," he said. "I like to think of it as we are spending money to educate. The average Joe on the street thinks of steel as 'Oh, hold my nose! It's that old, lethargic, polluting industry.' Thirty years ago that was true. Not any more. We have to get our great steel story out."[1]

John's right. Steel is the most recyclable product in the world. There is more steel recycled than paper, plastics, copper, and aluminum combined. You can build a house from steel derived from about eight old cars, using materials that are entirely recyclable, and save about a dozen trees. And that house will stand indefinitely. We want to get the facts about steel to consumers.

———■■■———

STRESSING LONG-TERM survival over short-term profitability; "sharing the pain" instead of lining the pockets of our executives; pushing decision-making authority down to the front-line worker; minimizing distinctions between managers and employees; paying people for their productivity . . . These aren't part of some revolutionary new management concept. They're components of a very simple and very straightforward business rationale—one that focuses employees on driving our bottom-line performance, and managers on removing obstacles from their path.

When I travel through our company, I can talk to employees doing work as diverse as drafting, accounting, production, or sales, and any one of them can tell me the level of profits their division has attained so far for the year. We've resisted the temptation to overcomplicate what our business is about. We know what's important.

From 1966 to 1996, Nucor Corporation grew at an annual compound rate of about 17 percent. Each and every year, we've turned a profit. And for twenty-five straight years, we've paid shareholders a dividend. Sure, there are companies that grow two, three, even four times as fast as we do in any given year. But more than a few of the dazzling meteors we saw flash across the skies have long since faded from view. Nucor, meanwhile, has gone on chalking up year after year of double-digit, profitable growth. So, if you hoped that Nucor would prove more intricate and extravagant, remember, keeping things simple works for us.

Epilogue: The Cure
for the Common MBA

W E   H A V E N ' T   H A D   much luck with the MBAs we've hired out of the top business schools. They've come to us, degree in hand, saying: "I'm ready to conquer the world." So we hired them and found they couldn't conquer the basics of managing a department.

Oh, they're smart enough. They're very good at finance and accounting. They can cite management theories, spout business buzzwords, and diagram models for every occasion. But they have a terrible time talking with an employee who is operating a machine. They just don't know how to relate to and lead people. They lack the basic communications skills.

I imagine Nucor isn't the only company to have had this experience. Something's definitely wrong here. The express purpose of business schools is to turn out competent, professional managers. But they don't. At least, not to my satisfaction.

Part of the problem, I'm sure, is that some MBAs enter the field of management for the wrong reasons. A management career should be about building a business that will survive and succeed over the long term. All too often, though, MBA students seem to focus on the short term, on balance sheet management, and on making deals.

In the late 1970s, for example, I was invited to the Harvard Business School to hear the first presentation of their new case study based on Nucor Corporation. The question posed in the case was: "Should Nucor continue to build mini-mills in other parts of the country?" We had three mini-mills operating at the time. Today, we have eight.

Well, something like 80 percent of the students concluded that Nucor should *not* go on building mini-mills. Most felt that we'd never be able to compete with the big steel companies.

After the class, I asked the professor: "Are your students always that conservative? Do they usually have that much trouble seeing what kinds of opportunities might be out there, long-term?"

He said, "They really aren't comfortable taking risks that aren't sure to pay off right away. Their idea of success is to get rich quick and retire."

I believe that the attitude among business school students is more entrepreneurial today than it was back then, and that's all to the good. Doing what's good for the business, long-term, should come somewhere ahead of personal enrichment on every manager's list of priorities. So I say to anyone who would pursue a career in management: Don't become a manager if all you want from your career is a quick buck. You'll never be very good at what you do. In fact, the business world would be better off without you.

I have little doubt, though, that many MBAs enter the management profession with admirable motives. They're intrigued by business. They're looking to give more than they receive. They want to *contribute*. But when they get out into the real world, they find that their schooling has not appropriately equipped them to meet the true demands of management.

That sounds like a condemnation of business schools. It is not. Not entirely. We forget, sometimes, that the "business school" is still in the experimental stage. It is an innovation of the latter twentieth century. What's more, it is predominantly an *American* innovation. Japan and Germany have relatively few business schools.

In my opinion, the business school is a noble experiment. It may prove a great success some day. All I am saying is that it has not proven a great success *yet*.

I would urge those who shape business school curricula, then, to consider two basic changes to how their institutions currently educate MBAs:

a) Revamp the core business school curriculum to make room for development of new management skills, especially in the area of communicating with employees;

b) Require at least a one-year, full-time management internship, preferably to be completed in a small business.

Positively influencing human behavior and performance is the most universal of management responsibilities. How can you expect managers to do that when they don't know how to connect to and communicate with people?

Business school curricula should *begin* with developing managers' ability to understand people and to effectively relate to them. Once MBA students have demonstrated mastery of people management basics, they could move on to tackling the "hard" skills and techniques required for their chosen management specialties.

Here are some of the subjects that might form the core of first-year MBA curricula:

- *Earning Employees' Trust and Loyalty*—Far too many managers have no clue how their employees feel or even what their people's work lives are like, day to day. Employees pick up on this lack of insight in a heartbeat, and that realization taints everything their managers say to them from that point forward. Conversely, employees clearly give the benefit of the doubt to managers whom they see as understanding "what's really going on" and "what we're really up against." That's only natural.

   I'd suggest, then, that every MBA candidate be required to spend at least a few weeks engaged in manual, clerical, and/or other forms of nonmanagement labor. Further, they should be required to keep a journal of their experiences—the kinds of problems they encounter, their frustrations, their successes, and so forth. They will find that what seems a small thing to them as managers often takes on great significance to them as employees.

   Developing managers should also contemplate the implicit and explicit commitments they will make to the people who work for them. They should understand their obligations under those commitments as well as the limitations of those obligations. And they should grasp the consequences of failing to be consistently trust-worthy.

- *Active Listening*—Listening is among the scarc-est of all human skills, in and out of manage-ment. Listening requires concentration, skill, patience, and a lot of practice.

  But such practice is a very sound investment of the developing manager's time. Real listening enables managers not only to hear what people say to them, but to sense what may be *behind* what is said (i.e., employees' emotions, assump-tions, biases). Better still, their reputation for competent listening will encourage others to bring them information.

  Listening proficiency is an immense advan-tage to any manager. No MBA should be sent forth into the business world without it.

- *The Hazards of Hierarchical Power*—Inexperi-enced managers tend to lean heavily on formal, hierarchical sources of authority. This is under-standable. They have not yet had the opportu-nity to develop other forms of authority such as experience, expertise, and seniority.

  The problem is, young managers don't often comprehend the hazards of hierarchical power. They do not understand that, by setting them-selves above and apart from their employees, they may actually be digging themselves into a hole. I think it is only fair, then, that we warn inexperienced managers of the hazards of hierarchical power.

- *Principles of Equitable Treatment*—Few managers receive much in the way of explicit instruction in the principles of equitable treatment of employees, either in business school or in the course of management development. All too often, managers fill that vacuum with their own self-serving precepts of what is equitable. A few common-sense principles, clearly stated and strongly advocated in the business schools, could make the business world a better, more equitable place for employees and managers alike.

The notion of an internship for managers has a precedent in medical education, of course. Doctors intern for a number of years before they are turned loose on the world. There ought to be a comparable transitional step in completing the requirements for an MBA. Further, that transition should focus on providing the management candidate hands-on experience. Any MBA who ventures into business with the intent of managing people should first develop his or her skills under the watchful guidance of an experienced manager.

The fact is, few business school professors have ever managed anything, and their lack of hands-on experience shows in their students. Medical school faculties, in contrast, are comprised of the best and most respected *practicing* physicians.

MBA candidates should preferably complete their internships within relatively small, self-contained operations, so they can perceive the operation in its entirety and grasp the overall dynamics of a business. People throughout the corporate world lament that other parts of their company don't understand them or what they do. They're usually right. It takes an extraordinary individual to understand aspects of a business to which he or she has never been exposed. We are expecting far too many managers to be extraordinary.

Some business schools, such as the Fuqua School of Management at Duke University, actively recruit practicing managers, engineers, and other experienced businesspeople into their MBA programs. This is certainly better than conferring MBAs onto those who complete course work but have never managed anyone or anything. But is it enough? Definitely not. A research study cited in a 1997 issue of *BusinessWeek* found that while 85 percent of business school deans say work experience should be an important consideration in evaluating prospective MBA students, applicants with extensive work experience were somewhat *less* likely, everything else being equal, to get into the most selective business schools than were candidates with no work experience.[1]

It is time for business schools to explicitly structure actual management time into the MBA curriculum. Nothing short of that will ensure that all of business school graduates emerge truly equipped to manage in the real world.

Meanwhile, I'll go on doing what I can to let business students know that the real world doesn't always match up to what they learn in their course work. I take a lot of phone calls from business students. It's fun. As they get over the shock of actually reaching me on the first phone call, there's a frantic rustling of papers, then they'll ask, "Um, can we have a copy of your mission statement?" I'll tell them we don't have one, but everyone at Nucor knows what we're trying to do. "Well, then, could you send me some of your job descriptions?" Nucor doesn't have job descriptions. "You don't have job descriptions either?" they say, amazed. "Wait until my professor hears this!"

I just hope business school professors are as ready to learn as are their students.

Notes

CHAPTER 1

1. "Bethlehem Steel CEO Gets Pay Raise of 37% Despite Profit Drop," *Wall Street Journal*, March 17, 1997.
2. "How Nucor Crawfordsville Works," *New Steel*, December 1995.
3. "Freedom and a Hell of a Lot More at Nucor," *New Steel*, Claude Riggin, July 1996.

CHAPTER 3

1. John Strohmeyer, *Crisis in Bethlehem: Big Steel's Struggle to Survive*, University of Pittsburgh Press, 1994.

CHAPTER 4

1. Special thanks to *New Steel* for its employee-focused article profiling Crawfordsville, in the December 1995 issue.
2. Ibid.
3. We can make a pretty strong case, incidentally, for the idea that working people are the real geniuses. A well-run integrated steel mill might produce about 700 tons of steel per employee each year, at a labor cost of roughly $100 per ton. Nucor's mini-mills annually produce about 2000 tons of steel per employee, at a labor cost of roughly $40 per ton. Our experience strongly suggests that when you ask employees to make most of the decisions, they can be more productive.
4. American Society for Training and Development, Information Resource Center.

CHAPTER 6

1. Peter F. Drucker, *The Practice of Management*, HarperCollins, 1986, pp. 231 and 234.

CHAPTER 8

1. *Webster's New Collegiate Dictionary*, Merriam-Webster Inc.

CHAPTER 9

1. "A Question for John Correnti," *The Charlotte Observer*, May 12, 1997.

EPILOGUE

1. "Getting into a Top B-School: Surprise, a Work Record Won't Help," *Business-Week*, April 15, 1997.

INDEX

INDEX